"Southern Gardenwalks leads one through a large and varied geographic area containing an even more abundant collection of horticultural treasures. Its knowledgeable and unbiased description of each destination enables one to quickly select those most suited to ones personal tastes. For those of us lacking the luxury of unlimited study and planning time, whether we seek the awe associated with a visit to one of the areas oldest and best known garden complexes such as Charleston's Magnolia Plantation, or prefer the less traveled roads to the many very worthy, but less known creations, this guide will leave us indebted for the knowledge, convenience and pleasure it will contribute to our trips."

—J. Drayton Hastie, Director
Magnolia Plantation and Gardens

Southern Gardenwalks

SOUTHERN GARDENWALKS

*A Guide to the Most
Beautiful Gardens of the South*

MARINA HARRISON
LUCY D. ROSENFELD

MICHAEL KESEND PUBLISHING · NEW YORK

Copyright 2000 by Marina Harrison, and Lucy D. Rosenfeld;
First publication 2000

Library of Congress Cataloging-in-Publication Data
Harrison, Marina, 1939–
    Southern Gardenwalks : a guide to the most beautiful
gardens of the south / Marina Harrison, Lucy D. Rosenfeld;
Illustrations by Lucy D. Rosenfeld.
        p. cm
        ISBN 0-935576-55-X
    1. Gardens--Southern States--Guidebooks. 2. Southern
States--Guidebooks. I. Rosenfeld, Lucy D., 1939– II. Title.
        SB466.U65 S65 2000
    712' 0975--dc21   00-25885

CONTENTS

PREFACE

This book invites garden lovers to join us in a search for beautiful and interesting sights. While we don't pretend to be horticulturists, botanists, or even to have very green thumbs ourselves, we do know an aesthetic treat when we see one.

As you may know from our previous guidebooks, we are inveterate walkers and connoisseurs of exceptional art and scenery. The gardens we have selected in our Southern region provide both natural and aesthetic pleasures. We describe in some detail our favorite gardens, which reflect the melting pot aspects of our nation, ranging in style from the most eccentric personal expressions to the traditional formal elegance found in European and Asian forms. Nor have we overlooked natural and wildflower preserves, which some people consider the best gardens of all. Also included are sculpture and architectural gardens; conservatories and indoor gardens; specialty gardens; colonial and plantation gardens; gardens for the disabled; Asian gardens; and gardens with great views, whose very settings make them special.

We have tried to introduce you to the various historic, multinational, and artistic garden designs in a section at the beginning of the book called "Thoughts on Garden Styles." At the end of the book is "Choosing an Outing," a guide that will help you select a garden to visit according to style or tradition.

Every garden in this book is open to the public on a more or less regular basis in season; we have not included gardens open only one day a year. While we cannot—in a useful, portable guide—fully describe every choice garden, we have given a thumbnail sketch of those you should not miss as you travel around the South.

We have spent wonderful days visiting every sort of garden in every season—on beautiful sunny days, as well as in pouring rain. Wherever we have gone, we have been given enthusiastic and helpful suggestions. Many people have directed us to gardens we might have overlooked, and others have recommended books and garden tours, and have even led us to hard-to-find places themselves. Among those we would like to thank are Jane Coe, Diana Green, Sophie

Rosenfeld and Matthew Affron, Catherine and Ray Stainback, Susan and Phil Harrison, and our always willing and enthusiastic husbands, Peter Rosenfeld and Jim Harrison. To Michael Kesend, we extend our thanks for his encouragement and the realization of our vision.

Gardens are, by definition, fragile. As living environments they are subject to the whims and changes of nature—and nurture. As we wrote this book, all the gardens we describe were in good condition and welcomed visitors. We hope you will find them as pleasing and carefully tended as we have.

GLOSSARY

Allée: a stately tree-lined avenue

Arboretum: a place where an extensive variety of trees are cultivated for scientific, educational, or ornamental purposes

Belvedere: a structure such as a summer house situated to command a view

Bosquet: a small grove or thicket

Botanical garden: a place where a wide variety of plants are cultivated for scientific, educational, or ornamental purposes

Butterfly garden: a garden in which flowers are specially chosen to attract butterflies

Classical garden: a formal garden whose aesthetic attitudes and values are embodied in ancient Greek and Roman design

Colonial (or plantation) garden: a garden designed or reconstructed in the colonial American style, with separate sections for flowers, fruit trees, vegetables, herbs, and various outbuildings

Conservatory: a greenhouse in which plants are arranged for aesthetic display and in carefully controlled climatic conditions

Cottage garden: a small, unpretentious garden featuring flowers and vegetables in a casual arrangement

Cup garden: a garden in the ancient Chinese tradition, in which an object is framed by its surroundings

Demonstration garden: a garden whose purpose is horticultural education

English garden: a naturalistic garden style first developed in eighteenth-century England, as compared with the more formal French style

Espalier: a fruit tree or shrub trained to grow flat against a wall, often in a symmetrical pattern

Folly: a whimsical garden structure that is decorative rather than useful

Formal garden: a garden in which nature is trained to adhere to geometric or other formal decorative principles

Gazebo: a free-standing roofed structure, usually with open sides, that provides a shady resting place in a garden

Grotto: a small cave or cavern, or an artificial structure made to resemble one

Ha-ha: a sunken hedge or moat that serves as a fence without impairing the view

Hydrophytic garden: an aquatic or water garden

Italianate garden: a garden in the Italian style often featuring classical elements, statuary, and fountains

Knot garden: elaborate planting of greenery, usually thyme or boxwood, following the patterns of knots

Maze: a garden labyrinth: an intricate, deliberately confusing, patterned network of hedges and pathways, designed to entertain

Naturalistic garden: a garden in which the design attempts to imitate nature in its free form, rather than to impose form upon it

Orangerie: a sheltered place such as a greenhouse, used particularly in cold climates, to grow oranges

Parterre: an ornamental flower garden whose beds and paths form a pattern

Pergola: an arbor or passageway with a roof or trellis on which climbing plants are trained to grow

Pleasure garden: a garden such as a flower garden or park, designed purely for enjoyment

Promenade: a place for strolling in a garden

Rock garden: a garden in which rocks and plants are arranged in a carefully designed, decorative scheme, often featuring Alpine plants

Shade garden: a garden featuring plants that grow best in shaded areas

Topiary garden: a garden in which live trees and shrubs are clipped into fanciful shapes

Water garden: a garden in which ponds, streams, and other water elements, as well as plants that grow at water sites, are an integral part of the overall design

Wildflower garden: usually a preserve, in which flowering plants grow in a natural, uncultivated state

Winter garden: a conservatory or other indoor garden that can be enjoyed all year

Xeriscope: a dry garden

Zen garden: a garden in the Japanese tradition designed for beauty and contemplation

THOUGHTS ON GARDEN STYLES

The Formal and Informal Garden

"Romanticism" is an idea which needed a classical mind to have it.
—*J.F. Shade (1898–1959)*

Among the fundamental questions that have defined landscape design in America and other Western countries is the issue of formal versus naturalistic gardens. Should a garden focus on structure and architecture or on its plantings? Should it be arranged in geometric patterns, or in a flowing, more random manner reflecting a natural landscape?

The formal approach has its cultural roots in the traditions of Italy and France. Formal gardens in the Italian and French style share important similarities. Both are regarded as architectural extensions of the house; both emphasize structure, symmetry, and classical motifs, such as statues and balustraded terraces; and in both, plants are considered subordinate to the overall design.

The first Italian gardens (as we know them today) appeared during the Renaissance, especially in the regions surrounding Florence and Rome, where some of the most important patrons, sculptors, and architects lived and worked. Villas were built as rural retreats from the city, much like their predecessors in antiquity. Their gardens, linking the house to the surrounding countryside, were designed to be ideal sites for contemplating and experiencing nature. At carefully chosen sites, viewers were invited to enjoy sweeping vistas of the formal layout and the countryside beyond.

The ideal Italian Renaissance garden—elegant, proportioned, and symmetrical—represented a harmonious balance between nature and architecture. Here nature was tamed and ordered into neatly clipped evergreens of laurel, box, and yew, shaped into elaborate mazes and borders. Stone and marble forms—colonnaded stairways, terraces, and statues depicting allegorical and mythological characters—were essential elements of this style. So, too, was water. The Villa d'Este at Tivoli, with its spectacular fountains, cascades, and basins—and amazing waterpowered mechanisms—is one of the most magnificent Renaissance gardens of all.

The Medici family of Florence helped introduce Italian garden designs to France, as did migrating Italian artisans and gardeners. The formal gardens of seventeenth-century France represented a new interpretation of these ideals. To a substantially greater degree than Italian gardens, these totally controlled landscapes symbolized humanity's mastery of the natural world.

Essential to French formal gardens were ornamental garden beds (parterres) fashioned from exquisitely shaped boxwood and yew. These intricate geometric compartments with squares, circles, and ovals were flawless in their symmetrical designs. They could be viewed from the formal reception rooms of the house overlooking them, or along an orderly grid of walkways. Sometimes complementing them were rows of small trees or shrubs shaped into topiary forms. (Topiaries in Italy tended to represent whimsical creatures, while those in France were strictly geometric and abstract.)

Versailles, the great masterpiece of André Le Nôtre, is certainly the most noted garden in the French style. Everything in it was laid out to symbolize the triumph of humanity (more specifically, Louis XIV or the Sun King) over nature, from its majestic proportions and perspectives, to the central axis leading to broad vistas, to the grand canals, fountains, and heroic statues.

In contrast to the formality and symmetry of the continental garden, the English Arcadian landscape was a dramatic return to nature. Influenced by romantic landscape painting and the glory of ancient ruins, English garden designers in the eighteenth century sought to recreate a sense of nature's free, wild beauty. Instead of the classical elegance of geometric perspective, orderly planting beds, walkways, and rectangular reflecting pools, the English garden turned to poetic disorder, to free-form designs, even to reconstructed ruins and grottos—in short, to the garden as a metaphor for romantic poetry and art. Its aim was the "picturesque."

"All gardening is landscape painting," remarked the first great English landscape designer, William Kent. It was Capability Brown and Humphrey Repton, however, who created the Arcadian landscapes of the great English country houses. In their designs the garden became landscape, a rolling vista that combined hills and fields, clumps of trees, rushing water, poetic lakes, and everywhere distant views. The flower garden was replaced by the beauties of landscape. There are "three aspects of landscape gardening," wrote William Shenstone, "the sublime, the beautiful, and the melancholy or pensive."

The "English garden" as we know it evolved from these poetic landscapes. The flower garden near the house made a comeback in the nineteenth century, replacing the vast green lawns just beyond the door. With a new emphasis on color and an abundance of apparently (though not at all) disordered plantings in mixed species, the glorious flowerbeds that we think of as English became popular. This style of informal "cottage garden" swept into fashion and could be seen everywhere—from the terraces of grand houses of Britain to Monet's gardens at Giverny. The return of flower gardens and the Victorian interest in the exotic and the extravagant led to increasing use of imported plants, rare flowers, and "the gardenesque"—a deliberately near-chaotic approach to landscape.

To Americans, gifted with spectacular landscapes of a "natural paradise," most thoughts of French formality seemed irrelevant. As Americans first moved beyond their careful, colonial-style gardens into the realm of larger pleasure gardens, many were surely influenced by the English style. Americans with large estates, as well as those planning the first public parks, tried to incorporate natural landscape wonders into their own garden designs. Picturesque gardens were nestled into areas like the magnificent Palisades along the Hudson River, their dramatic settings adding to both design and ambiance.

As the great era of wealth in the late nineteenth century brought increased travel abroad, America's newly rich familiarized themselves with the elegant French and Italian landscape. Castles rivaling those of Europe were constructed in places like Newport or Philadelphia. Surrounding them were great formal gardens, patterned after Versailles or other grand continental wonders. To the owners of the American places, the French garden seemed the epitome of grandeur, the free-form English garden a less elegant option.

As you visit gardens today, you'll find distinct examples of both continental formality and the English "picturesque." But in many cases, particularly in gardens designed in the more recent past, you'll see a mixture of styles and influences that is typical of so many of our contemporary arts. Borrowing liberally from the varied ideas of the past, today's gardens might include formality and fountains, as well as free-form planting beds and abstract contemporary sculpture. Exotic plantings, so prized by Victorians, might grow alongside a traditional Roman wall, or a geometric reflecting pool might be edged with contemporary tile. The postmodern emphasis on using elements from diverse sources has not escaped the world of landscape design. Thus, the debate between English informality and continental formality has all but passed into garden history, like the artificial grotto, the ha-ha, and the topiary maze.

The Colonial and Plantation Garden

"Let every house be placed if the Person pleases in the middle of its plot so that there may be ground on each side for Gardens or Orchards, or fields, so that it may be a green Country Towne . . . and will always be wholesome."

—*William Penn*

Colonial gardens are an important part of America's cultural heritage, and one of its most delightful. Scattered about from New England throughout the South, they represent a particular time in our history. Whether authentic seventeenth- and eighteenth-century gardens, replicas, or simply newer interpretations of a basic style, they all share certain characteristics, with some variation. More formal than not (without being necessarily "grand"), they are ordered, geometric, and often symmetrical. Most are enclosed and intimate. Their organized structure reflects the needs and perspectives of a culture that prized order, balance, and economy.

The early settlers had a pragmatic approach to gardening, whether they were facing the harsh winters of Massachusetts, or the milder climate of Virginia. First, it was essential to enclose each household compound to keep out animals, wild or domestic. Within a fence or stone wall was a well-planned arrangement that emphasized function, rather than aesthetics, without compromising overall harmony and charm. The location of the house, its outbuildings and connecting "yards," and planted areas were carefully sited for best drainage and exposure. Each had its specific purpose. Between the house and outbuildings was the "dooryard," where animals were shorn, soap made, or wool dyed. This rustic spot was hardly a place for much greenery, except for a few shade trees (which were also useful as places to attach pulleys and lift heavy objects).

Each family maintained a basic garden and orchard to serve its needs. These formal plantings were often wedged in small areas between the house, yards, sheds, barns, meadows, and pastures. At first, necessity dictated planting vegetables and fruit shrubs and trees, rather than flowers. (During the eighteenth century, gardens became less utilitarian and often included decorative plants, as well as edibles.) Orchards contained large fruit trees, such as apples; but pears, peaches, apricots, and plums were arranged in borders or espaliers closer to the house. Herbs used for cooking were planted in simple, rectangular plots next to the house, or were sometimes mixed in with other plants. Physicians sometimes kept a "physic garden," or botanic garden, to provide the proper curative herbs for their patients.

On large colonial southern plantations it was especially essential to create kitchen gardens and orchards, since they were often isolated from towns and villages. And given a more agreeable climate than that found in New England, plentiful varieties of English plants thrived there. According to Robert Beverly, who in 1705 wrote *History of the Present State of Virginia*, "A Kitchen-Garden don't thrive better or faster in any part of the Universe than there. They have all the Culinary Plants that grow in England, and in far greater perfection, than in England."

Most colonial gardens were arranged in neat, rectangular blocks bordered by boxwood (especially in the South) or other decorative plants. Separating these geometric, cultivated areas were brick or stone paths. The more elaborate gardens might also include a central azalea path aligned with the main door of the house and leading to a vista, stone bench, or statue. On either side of the walk were raised plots (for better drainage), usually arranged in symmetrical fashion. While vegetables and small fruits were kept in designated areas, ornamental plants surrounded the more important walkways. Sometimes edible plants and flowers were mixed in together, creating formal geometric designs.

In Virginia and other parts of the South, colonial—or plantation—gardens tended to be larger and more elaborate than in the North. With large-scale introduction of slavery into the southern colonies, manor houses were built, surrounded by often grand landscaped settings. The Virginia Tidewater plantations were particularly picturesque. Poised on rolling terrain high above rivers or canals, they enjoyed sweeping views over the surrounding landscape. While manor houses were usually set so as to command the best vistas, the gardens themselves were often located on descending terraces, in a theatrical arrangement reminiscent of Renaissance Italian and seventeenth-century English gardens. A large, enclosed, rectangular garden near the house featured vegetables and herbs planted in symmetrical patterns. Other terraces might include a bowling green (popular in mid-seventeenth-century English gardens), boxwood parterres with flowers or vegetables, and fruit orchards. There would also be English-style parklands, complete with grazing animals, adding to the bucolic character of the site. Among the greatest of such plantation gardens is the Governor's Place in Williamsburg, famous for its elegant eighteenth- century gardens (and a popular tourist attraction to this day). Another is Gunston Hall, an example of a well-designed twentieth-century recreation featuring a stately arrangement of boxwoods growing in neat, geometric hedges.

Thomas Jefferson, who along with George Washington was one of the most famous colonial gardeners of all, had an abiding interest in horticulture, garden design, and botany—and a fundamental belief that the strength of the country lay in its agrarian society. He surrounded his extraordinary estate, Monticello, with vegetable plots (where he conducted various experiments), flowerbeds, and orchards. Monticello and Washington's Mt. Vernon are examples of the colonial style at its grandest; but, still, they were created in basically the same spirit as the simplest colonial garden, emphasizing order, harmony, and the balance of pleasure and usefulness.

The Walled Garden

"A garden inclosed is my sister, my spouse; a spring shut up, a fountain sealed. Thy plants are an orchard of pomegranates with pleasant fruits."
                        —from The Song of Solomon

Throughout history gardens have been seen as different, idealized worlds in which we create an orderly and beautiful environment cut off from tumultuous reality. Thus, of course, they must be enclosed. Most gardens, in fact, are surrounded in some way—separated from the wild, the urban, the public, the unknown. In this way gardens are like beautifully framed paintings. Such divisions between the wild and intrusive, and the cultivated and the private create the sense of specialness and secrecy that characterizes an enclosed space. The "secret garden" is a concept that is undeniably inviting.

Artificial boundaries for gardens—when they are not naturally surrounded by geographical borders—are most often created by walls, hedges, or fences. Whether the border is formed by high boxwood hedges or medieval stone walls, trellis fences or rows of evergreens, the "framing" of the garden is found all over the world, and throughout garden history.

The walled garden is the most private, for walls—whether of stone or hedge—can be high and impenetrable. Their origins are long in the past, when they kept out human and animal intruders and protected those within. In many cultures the enclosed garden, designed for both useful growing and pleasing contemplation, was a practical or an aesthetic choice. Thus the enclosed gardens of some civilizations—such as Egyptian and medieval Christian—were also metaphors for religious belief. (Walled gardens of the Middle Ages, for example, were thought to symbolize freedom and beauty with precisely set boundaries.)

Beautiful enclosed gardens can be seen in paintings from Egyptian and Roman walls, in Persian miniatures, and in the cloisters of medieval buildings. Trellis-fenced gardens appear in Renaissance art; the great classical gardens of France and England used both hedges and fences to enclose parts of their elaborate landscape designs. Boxwood, evergreen, and other living borders were common in gardens ranging from ancient Rome to colonial America, their carefully tended shapes creating dense hedgerows and geometric patterns.

Many of these garden boundaries were not just utilitarian borders to surround the plantings, but were integral parts of the garden design. Medieval walls featured carvings, patterned stonework, delicate espaliered trees or climbing plants, and carved stone blossoms reflecting the blooms within the garden. Some of the thick hedge borders of the most complex European gardens were cut into topiary designs, making the garden "walls" fantastic in shape and illusion.

American enclosed gardens date to colonial times, when their walls kept out the frightening wilderness. Many early American gardens have high brick walls and matching paths whose subtle deep red contrasts delightfully with the dark shiny greens of ivy and boxwoods. Versions in the United States of European cloisters and Victorian "cottages" included walled gardens. Our great nineteenth-century estates feature many enclosed garden areas, in which marble and granite not only provide a backdrop for plantings and sculpture, but create both color and texture in themselves. Espaliered fruit trees, climbing roses, ivy, wisteria, and trumpet vines are among the many popular plantings that can be seen covering the walls of enclosed gardens.

Today the walled garden is often in the middle of a city. Urban gardeners use stone or brick walls in imaginative and contemporary ways, sometimes combining sculpture, falling water, and environmental design. Some of the smallest, but most appealing walled gardens today are the "vest-pocket" parks in our cities.

Clearly, the concept of the enclosed garden is still valid; its plantings and design may be symbolic or practical or purely aesthetic, but the walled garden remains a special, magical space, serene and cut off from the world outside.

The Topiary Garden

"And all these [flowers] by the skill of your Gardener, so comelily and orderly placed in your borders and squares and so intermingled, that one looking thereon, cannot but wonder to see, what Nature, corrected by Art, can do."

—William Lawson,
A New Orchard and Garden, *1618*

Topiary, the ancient art of shaping plants into living sculptures, has brought charm, whimsy, and surprise to many a garden over the centuries. The term comes from the Latin *toparius*, referring to a gardener who specializes in carving plants; for it is such a gardener who, with the skill and vision of an artist, can transform an ordinary landscape into a delightful living tableau, adding both elegance and fun to the landscape. Because of its many possibilities of expression, topiary art has appealed to gardeners of all kinds, including the most eccentric, who find it an amusing outlet for their imaginations.

The topiary tradition comes with a wealth of sculpted plant shapes and designs. Shrubs and trees are pruned, clipped, cut, coaxed, and styled (sometimes on wire frames) into fanciful animals, mythological creatures, or elegant geometric forms. Yew, privet, hemlock, boxwood, and ivy—to name some of the most popular plants used—can be fashioned into peacocks, roosters, dragons, and centaurs, as well as pyramids, globes, arches, and decorative scalloped hedges. Some topiary gardens feature entire sequential scenes: for example, a leafy foxhunt or a flotilla of ships. Others are created on an intimate scale and might include potted topiary that can be moved about, or brought indoors.

Topiary gardens are not limited to green sculptures, however. There are also espalier gardens, knot gardens, parterres, and mazes. The espalier is a plant trained into an open, flat pattern to create a two-dimensional effect. The branches of shrubs and trees—often fruit trees such as pear, peach, and apple trees—are bent and pruned into intricate, delicate motifs to adorn walls and other vertical surfaces.

Knot gardens are level beds whose designs are made from the intertwining patterns of herbs and hedges. (Today's versions sometimes include flowers and pebbles as well.)

The *parterre* (French for "on the ground") is a variation of the knot garden. Usually on a larger scale, its designs are more fluid, with arabesques, open scrolls, or *fleurs de lis*. Patterns are created by using carefully clipped dwarf hedges, flowers, grass, and colored stones.

The maze—one of the more delightful topiary forms—is like a life-sized puzzle. It is made of a network of connecting hedges and paths intended to amuse through surprise and confusion. In its earlier forms, in eighteenth-century Europe, the maze sometimes included hidden water games and sprays that were meant to catch the unsuspecting visitor by surprise, or well hidden lovers' benches at the very center.

The history of topiary gardens shows us that, though they were highly popular from Roman times until the eighteenth century, they are much more rare today in contemporary gardens (though in European gardens of the past you will find many restored topiaries).

The earliest recorded topiary garden seems to have come about in ancient Rome. Around 100 A.D. the younger Pliny drew a distinction between the beauties of nature—beloved by the Romans—and the beauties of a cultivated garden. Pliny wrote long letters describing the gardens he had laid out at his Tuscan estate. Distinguishing between art and nature, he commented that the beauty of the landscape was owing to nature, while the beauty of his garden was owed to "art."

In describing in detail his plantings and garden design, Pliny indicated that his gardeners had employed what we know of today as topiary gardens. His paths, he wrote, were lined with boxwood hedges "and in between grass plots with box trees cut into all kinds of different shapes, some of them being letters spelling out the name of the owner or of the gardener who did the work." Interspersed with these topiary delights were white marble statues, obelisks, pillars, and seating areas.

A friend of Emperor Augustus named C. Matius was responsible for the invention of the topiary garden. Matius, according to Pliny's uncle, had invented the cutting of trees into various shapes around 5 B.C. (Don't be surprised by the sophistication of ancient Roman gardening; they had been grafting fruit trees, for example, for generations by the time Pliny made his gardens!)

We next hear of the topiary garden in medieval times, when the Flemish, in particular, favored small clipped evergreens (box or yew, as today) trained into tiers. (You can see a somewhat later example of the Flemish topiary in Pieter Breughel's *Spring*.) But unlike the Romans, the Flemish apparently only clipped their evergreens in simple ways, rather than into the elaborate designs described by Pliny.

French medieval gardeners developed the espalier in their walled cities where there was little room for orchards. The fact that espaliers required little space and bore their fruit early and abundantly was a great asset during those harsh times. Later, espaliers became popular as purely ornamental features in French gardens.

The first mazes were also developed in France in the Middle Ages, inspired by the medieval belief that a penitent soul might crawl on his hands and knees to imitate the path of earthly travail and thus gain heavenly grace.

Topiary art came thoroughly into fashion in the Italian Renaissance, when all of the arts and their illusionary qualities were so admired, and when so many classical and ancient styles were revived. A Renaissance gentleman named Leon Batista Alberti described the principles of garden design in the fifteenth century. Among his many pieces of advice (on a wide range of architectural and landscaping subjects) was to select sites with "a view of cites, land and sea, a spreading plain, and the known peaks of the hills and mountains." He recommended cool shell-covered grottoes, groves of fruit trees, and box-bordered paths and topiary work. "The gardeners of ancient times," he said, "flattered their patrons by writing their names in letters formed in box and other odorous herbs." We can see examples of the elaborate gardens of the fifteenth and sixteenth centuries (such as those described by Alberti) in engravings and paintings from France and Italy and England.

In fact, in Queen Elizabeth I's England in the sixteenth century, topiary designs, knot gardens, and mazes became quite fashionable at the palaces and castles of the aristocracy. At Sudely Castle in Gloucestershire, topiary yew hedges included small, doorlike openings for sheltering during England's sudden and frequent rain storms; Elizabeth's hunting lodge had both a knot garden and flat-cut hedges that are said to have been used for drying "linen, cloathes and yarne!" Among the designs used in Elizabethan gardens were "cockle shells," "beestes," "men armed in the field, ready to give battle," "swift-running greyhounds," "pretty pyramides," and "little turrets with bellies." Later English gardens featured "outdoor rooms" in which the lawn was the carpet and the topiary the "furniture."

France became a center of formal gardens under the Bourbon kings. In the seventeenth century the art of topiary was apparently *de rigueur* in the great formal settings of the French chateaux. Extravaganzas of all kinds characterized French Baroque court life; not the least of which were the elaborate pavilions and topiary designs. These included living plant decorations in the shapes of animals and people, sailing ships, and birds, as well as complex arrangements based on medieval dance patterns, parterres, three-part patterns, criss-crossed walks, mazes, and other features to entertain the lords and ladies who strolled through them.

But the craze for topiary gardens came to an end. In 1728 a French garden architect and writer (Alexandre Le Blond) wrote disparagingly, ". . . at present nobody gives into these trifles [topiary gardens] in France, how well soever they may be kept. . . . We choose rather a plain regularity less clutter'd and confus'd, which indeed looks much more noble and great." Rousseau's dedication to the principles of naturalism and informality and "the simple life" added to the dislike for the artificial topiary design. Instead, a new emphasis on natural beauty replaced the intricate formal gardens of the Baroque.

Visits to stately homes of Britain and chateaux of France will still often include historic topiary gardens and mazes. But in the United States, where we do not have the tradition in our past, they are more of a rarity. However, we have found several for your enjoyment. Read on!

The Conservatory Garden

"There is an inherent wonderful fascination in being able, in the middle of winter, to open the window of a salon and feel a balmy spring breeze instead of the raw December or January air. It may be raining outside, or the snow may be falling in soft flakes from a black sky, but one opens the glass doors and finds oneself in an earthly paradise that makes fun of the wintry showers."
—*Princess Mathilde de Bonaparte, 1869*

The idea of collecting, nurturing, and displaying plants in an enclosed, controlled environment is an ancient one. The first greenhouses may have been built by the Romans to protect the exotic plants they found during their military campaigns in distant lands. The emperor Nero's *specularium* (for so this type of Roman structure was called) contained his much loved cucumbers, which he could thus enjoy throughout the year. Over the course of human history plants have been gathered, arranged, and housed for many reasons—from the most pragmatic to aesthetic, spiritual, scientific or even whimsical. And their artificial habitats—from the specularium to the conservatory—have evolved considerably.

The earliest indoor gardens functioned both as places to display plants and to store and protect them from the sometimes harsh European winters. Ornamental plants were admired and often regarded as "trophies" won during victorious battles. (The taste for unusual flora existed at least as far back as ancient Egypt, when royal gardeners were routinely sent to other countries to gather rare species.) Crusaders and later many explorers came home with unfamiliar varieties, which required careful tending in controlled environments.

In sixteenth-century England and France it became fashionable to maintain decorative citrus trees, and *orangeries* came into being. In the elegant estates of the time these winter gardens were *de rigueur*. During the coldest months orange and lemon trees in large tubs were placed in neat rows inside glass-walled chambers, mostly for show. Some were on a very grand scale; indeed, the 9,000-square-foot orangerie at Heidelberg Castle in 1619 included more than 400 trees, many of which were at least 25 feet high!

But the real "botanic" gardens filled with rare plants—both indoor and outdoor—came into being as a result of a new interest in the spiritual and scientific dimensions of the plant kingdom. The Garden of Eden was actually the inspiration for the botanic gardens of the sixteenth century. After the discovery of the New World's natural life, the first notion arose of a *hortus inclusis*, a gathering of all the plants that had been dispersed from that biblical paradise. Exotic plants brought back from voyages around the world formed the basis for the first botanic gardens at Leiden, Padua, and Montpellier. In the next century others were started in Paris, London, and Uppsala, Sweden.

Most of these early gardens were arranged in squares, divided into quadrants representing the four corners of the earth (in those days that meant Asia, Africa, Europe, and America). The quadrants were then divided into parterres, with grass walks dividing them. Each plant was carefully labeled; the botanic garden became a "living encyclopedia" of Creation. (It was believed, in fact, that the visitor who spent time contemplating in such a place, might regain his or her lost innocence and even gain insight into the "mind of God.")

By the seventeenth century, theologians upset this easy method of finding Paradise. (They looked at zoos—established for the same reason—and saw no Peaceable Kingdoms ensuing.) Some great thinkers believed that the natural wilderness was closer to the original than these highly organized settings. And there were problems of a more practical nature: for example, which climate did the Garden of Eden have? Plants from so many different climes could not grow in the same place at the same temperature. The botanic garden as a place of science was created; it featured indoor and outdoor areas devoted to climatic differences, propagation, and the survival of species.

In their capacity as "laboratories" for scientific study, botanic gardens and, particularly, greenhouses, became places to grow plants for medicinal purposes. During the seventeenth and eighteenth centuries botanists traveled to the New World on merchant ships to identify and gather species of possible medicinal or other scientific value. John Bartram, among the most famous of these botanists, discovered many valuable tropical plants in his scientific expeditions abroad. (He was, by the way, a member of Captain James Cook's scientific expedition in 1772.)

The emphasis on greenhouses and imported rarities from all over the world also had an artistic effect: the concept of a "museum" of plants. The early botanic garden became a collection of exotic and fascinating individual plants, set out for easy enjoyment and identification, rather than a larger, overall form of environmental or artistic beauty. (As we will see below, these diverse aims have been admirably united in the botanic gardens of today.)

One of the first great botanical gardens in the United States was the Elgin Botanic Garden in New York City, where Rockefeller Center is today. Started in 1801, it occupied a huge area with a conservatory featuring scientifically identified plants. The garden—then in "the wilds" of upper Manhattan—was surrounded by a belt of trees and a great stone wall. Needless to say, it did not survive the city's expansion.

But in 1824 a Belgian horticulturist named André Parmentier came to New York and built the Brooklyn Botanic Garden. One of its most popular aspects was a tower from which visitors could see the gardens and surrounding area with a bird's-eye view. Parmentier's wonderful gardens still exist today and can be visited.

Another such enterprise was begun only 29 years after Washington became the capital of the United States (in 1820), when a group of amateur scientists founded a similar enterprise there. Although it lasted for only about 18 years before it ran out of funds, the idea of a national botanic garden was taken up again in 1842.

Plans for a new garden were encouraged by the 1838–42 commercial expedition of Captain Charles Wilkes (the model for Captain Ahab, by the way). He had circumnavigated the globe with 440 men and six ships (one of which must have been needed just to carry home the 10,000 plant variety of seeds, dried samples, and live plants he collected from all over the world). A federally funded national botanic garden was finally built in 1842. In 1849 it was moved to its present location and can be visited today in all its splendor.

As indoor gardens have had a variety of functions over the ages, so, too, have they evolved stylistically. The earliest greenhouses contained little glass; indeed, it is likely that Romans used sheets of mica instead to allow the sun to filter in. With improved technology, particularly during the Industrial Age, greenhouses became all glass structures and took on new shapes. While eighteenth-century orangeries and conservatories had had extensive windows but conventional roofs, in the nineteenth century they began to be built with domed roofs. Theorists had discovered that the form of roof best suited for the admission of the sun's rays was hemispherical. Because of the development of iron frames and glazed roofs it was now possible to build greenhouses that looked like what we now think of as "conservatories" (and what we imagine when we inevitably read about them in Victorian novels). These elegant and fanciful structures culminated with Sir Joseph Paxton's famous Crystal Palace, inaugurated as the main attraction at the First International Exhibition in Hyde Park, London, in 1851. Greeted with great enthusiasm, its enormous success helped stimulate the building of conservatories everywhere, including the United States. More elaborate than greenhouses, conservatories contained plants primarily chosen for their showy effect.

The Water Garden

"Any garden ornament or piece of architecture mirrored in water receives an addition to its dignity by the repetition and continuation of upright line."
—Gertrude Jekyll, 1901

Water has embellished gardens around the world since the earliest civilizations. Not only has it been used in gardens for practical reasons, but also for pure pleasure and decoration. The effects of water on the senses are varied and fascinating: it can delight, charm, soothe, cool, stimulate, and excite. Through its magical powers of illusion and reflection, it can create an environment of mystery and even surprise. Natural sources of water—streams, brooks, or waterfalls—as well as artful canals, pools, or fountains have been focal points in gardens over the ages.

The Egyptians were among the first who recognized the importance of "decorative water" in garden design. Ancient tomb paintings depict gardens with rectangular pools, lilies, lotus, and papyrus. Not only were these basins of water practical—they were used to irrigate the surroundings—but they were also refreshingly appealing in the parched lands.

The pleasure-loving Romans copied these early models in their own gardens, adding more sophisticated elements, such as elaborate fountains and canals. The fabled garden of Pliny the Younger included (according to his nephew) "a semicircular bench of white marble shaded with a vine which is trained on four small pillars of marble. Water, gushing through several little pipes from under this bench . . . falls on to a stone cistern underneath, from whence it is received into a fine polished marble basin, so artfully contrived that it is always full without overflowing." It seems that at mealtime plates of food were placed on the water, so they could float from one person to the next.

Water, revered by the Persians as the essence of life, was the chief element in their paradise gardens. These magnificent, enclosed oases with fountains, tiled pools, and intricate water channels provided a delicious respite in a torrid climate. Formal and geometric, they usually included rows of stately cypress trees and scented roses, irrigated by underground tunnels.

Water gardens reached some of their highest level of artistry in those created by the Moors of medieval Spain. Such magnificent and lavish gardens as those in the Alhambra were intricately planned by some of the most sophisticated designers of all time. These masterful hydraulic engineers/artists used ingenious techniques to channel precious water from distant mountain springs through elaborate tunnels to palaces and courtyards. The gardens were thus filled with the sight and sound of water continuously flowing (and recycled) through fountains, marbled channels, and basins.

The rest of Europe (which, during the Middle Ages had confined its gardens to relatively modest cloisters with small wells and fountains) saw a rebirth of the water garden during the Renaissance, especially in Italy. Along with a renewed interest in antiquities came a fascination with science and the study of such basic elements as water; water became a central focus of Italian villa gardens. Amid the waters of elegant fountains and graceful pools, and even inside mysterious grottoes, Italian designers placed statues depicting mythological characters—ranging from river gods and gorgons to Venus and Neptune surrounded by nymphs and dolphins. Amazing water-powered machines and animated ornaments graced some villa gardens; the fabled Villa d'Este, one of the most dazzling water gardens of all time (it still delights visitors today) displayed spectacular aquatic fireworks in addition to its other exquisite garden features.

Fountains were used most lavishly in seventeenth-century French gardens. At Versailles, for example, the master designer André le Nôtre (along with an army of artists and engineers) channeled water through myriad dams, falls, pools, cascades, and an especially long canal where mock naval battles were occasionally held to amuse the courtiers. Le Nôtre's designs for Versailles became a standard by which numerous other formal gardens were (and are still) measured.

Romantic English gardens used water in a less artificial way; instead of the grand geometric, formal pools and fountains of the French, they featured meandering streams and rivers surrounded with naturalistic plantings and graceful garden paths. Some of the great Capability Brown's designs called for picturesque garden lakes, created by dammed streams and massive excavations.

Of course, the "natural" use of water—so favored in the Romantic era—had long been featured in the gardens of the Far East. In classical Chinese and Japanese gardens water, regarded as a vital ingredient, appeared almost always in an entirely naturalistic way. But water in Asian gardens also had symbolic significance; for example, both the sight and the sound of water in Japanese gardens is part of the aesthetic importance of their traditional gardens.

Today, water gardens have been inspired by these varied historic and cultural traditions and reinterpreted to accommodate contemporary needs and tastes. As you visit gardens that feature water designs, you will perhaps identify some of these stylistic elements.

The Rock Garden

"It may appear at first that the collection of stones, etc., is designed to appear wild and irregular, little Art would be required in its construction; but this is so far from being the case, that perhaps, rockwork is more difficult to design and execute than any other kind of garden scenery."

—Jane Loudon, c. 1930

We take rock gardens for granted nowadays, enjoying the combination of hard, surprising stone and delicate, careful plantings. Many a rocky American hillside is planted these days with wildflowers and alpine specialties, and some such gardens are even created from the start.

But the rock garden does not have as long a history as most of the designs and styles of gardens we describe. In fact, the rock garden dates to 1777 when Sir Joseph Banks, a British naturalist (and President of the Royal Society some years later), visited Iceland. On a twelve-day hike to a volcanic mountain in Iceland, Banks collected the lava from the volcano's last eruption five years before. (He used it for ballast for his ship on the return to Britain.)

When he got home, he presented the hardened lava to the Apothecaries' Garden in Chelsea, where it was combined with piles of stone from the old walls of the Tower of London, discarded bricks, and various other types of stone. Plants began to grow all over this huge and motley mound of rock.

Within 50 years, rock gardens were popular in Britain. Jane and John Loudon, noted writers on all subjects of gardening, described "rockwork" as fragments of rock "thrown together in an artistic manner, so as to produce a striking and pleasing effect, and to serve as a nest or repository" for a variety of plants. Rock gardens are more difficult to design than they look, they warned their readers. As the "cluttered" garden (much like the Victorian parlor) soon replaced the expansive, airy stretches of the previous era, the rock garden with its many composite parts became more and more popular.

Among the early designs in private gardens for rockeries, as they were known, were an imitation Swiss mountain scene made of white marble to simulate snow, and a naturalistic rocky hollow made from an abandoned quarry. Plants for these original gardens varied from traditional British ornamental shrubs and flowers to imported specimens, originating from rocky hillsides in other countries.

By mid-century many English rock gardens were devoted entirely to Alpine plants in the Swiss style, even though the plants' native habitat on high, snowy mountains could not easily be transplanted to Britain. Advice proliferated on caring for such plants—described as "low, bushy, and evergreen" and "tiny and elfin"—and on how to design the rockeries. Before long, the rock garden became synonymous with the Alpine garden and a fashionable addition to many a country estate, where miniature mountains, gorges, valleys, waterfalls, and bridges appeared.

The Alpine garden was the subject of intense interest to botanists and gardeners who traveled the world in search of rare plants that adapted well to their stony surroundings. The designs for such gardens were described by Reginald Farrer in "My Rock Garden." He wrote derisively that there were three common ideas for rock gardens: the "Almond Pudding scheme," which has spiky pinnacles of limestone jutting up among the plants; the "Dog's Grave," with a pudding shape but its stones laid flat; and the "Devil's Lapful," which contains cartloads of bald, square-faced boulders dropped about anywhere, with plants dropped in between them. He preferred a naturalistic setting. (And so did many later garden designers, who went so far as to use imitation rocks to create "lifelike" landscapes.)

Today, the Alpine idea is still popular, but it is no longer an imitative or confining design. There is great freedom of idea and layout in the American rock gardens we have visited. Many combine the naturalistic features of a rocky terrain (with the huge boulders common to our part of the world) and a judicious use of stone walls and stairways and other rocky additions. The plantings in these gardens range widely from imported Alpine delicacies to plants that lend themselves to falling over stone walls. Raised beds, stone pools, and tiny waterfalls are among the elements you might find.

The Asian Garden

A lonely pond in age-old stillness sleeps,
Apart, unstirred by sound or motion till
Suddenly into it a little frog leaps . . .
                                    —Basho (1644–94)

Gardens of the Orient were the first to become living artistic statements. Closely aligned with the religious beliefs of Buddhism, Taoism, and Shintoism, Chinese and Japanese gardens were places of meditation and renewal. In an attempt to tame nature's wildness, deliberately placed trees and plants were combined with materials of long-lasting value, like wood, sand, and stone. Each element of the garden was symbolic, designed for spiritual awareness as its owners strolled through it.

Chinese "cup gardens"—ranging in size from picturesque lakes surrounded by hills to small stone areas with a bonsai (artificially pruned, miniature tree) in the center—were among the first symbolically designed Asian gardens. The earliest cup garden is believed to have been created by the great landscape painter and poet, Wang Wei (699–759 A.D.) during the T'ang Dynasty. It was Wang Wei who first articulated the close relationship of the Chinese garden to art, poetry, and spirituality.

If you look at a traditional scroll painting of a Chinese landscape, in fact, it is hard to know which art is imitating which. The great Chinese gardens have the ambiance of paintings, while the paintings seem inextricably bound up with the delicately designed traditional garden. Harmonious in design, the Chinese landscape is distinctive, with its careful balance of leaning trees and craggy rocks, arched bridges over reflective water, and gentle flowering plants.

The cup garden was surrounded (like the inside of a cup) by a wall or a hedge, or other barrier in order to provide isolation from the chaos of the outside world. Within its boundaries, the cup garden drew the visitor's attention to accents—a particular plant or stone or body of water. The garden's purpose was introspection and privacy, using an artistic design and symbolism to bring close communication and union with nature and its forces.

The symbolic elements and design of ancient Chinese gardens strongly influenced the Japanese, who went on to create elaborate and exquisite gardens of their own. The Japanese stroll garden also became a place for introspection, an orderly, aesthetic environment where balance, beauty, and harmony mirrored the proper harmony of the soul.

There is little that is accidental or uncalculated in a Japanese garden. Carefully placed, asymmetrical plantings, such as bamboo and katsurra trees, ferns, delicate iris, and lilies grow among symbolic settings. These important elements range from free-form ponds that reflect the sky, to statuary such as small deities or cranes (representing wisdom and long life), to raked sand (representing the ocean's tides), to carefully placed rocks and small stones (suggesting the earth's natural forms), to tiny islands in the pond (symbolizing clouds). Small buildings such as the familiar Japanese teahouse provide a haven of peace and beauty. To the Shintoists, spirits inhabit all natural phenomena, and the Japanese garden suggests no less than heaven on earth.

Southeast Asian gardens share many of the same designs and ideas, but in Thailand and Burma, for example, there is greater freedom from the precise symbolism of the Japanese. Though not as burdened by the meaning of each rock and bamboo shoot, these gardens are also spiritual sanctuaries adorned with sculptured deities, including small Buddhas set amid the greenery and flowers.

The Asian garden stunned and delighted Westerners who traveled to the East. In the seventeenth and eighteenth centuries many aspects of Chinese artistry—including garden design and exotic plants—began to appear in European gardens and subsequently in America.

Today, in addition to many great Chinese and Japanese gardens carefully maintained in the United States, we also find Oriental plantings and landscape design intermixed with the more Western styles of many of our American gardens. Among the elements adopted in our own gardens are numerous exotic trees (ranging from Asian magnolias and rhododendrons to Japanese flowering cherries) and many flowers, including species of jasmine, poppies, azaleas, and lilies.

But even more obvious to our Western eyes are the elements of Asian design that have crept into our own formal and informal gardens: trickling water and delicate lily ponds, small arched bridges and waterfalls, "living still lifes" of stones and foliage so prized in Asian design, and garden areas created for meditation and harmony with nature.

GARDENS TO VISIT

A L A B A M A

Birmingham
Gadsden
Huntsville
Mobile
Montgomery
Theodore

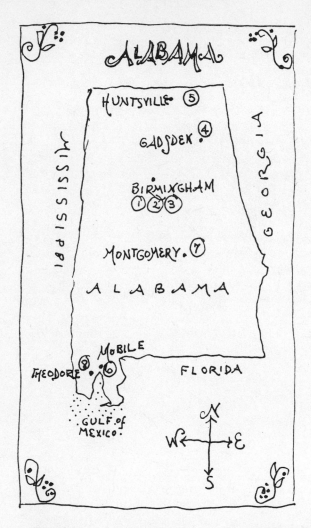

1. Birmingham: Arlington House and Garden
2. Birmingham: Birmingham Museum of Art, Charles W. Ireland Sculpture Garden
3. Birmingham: Birmingham Botanical Gardens
4. Gadsden: Noccalula Falls Botanical Gardens
5. Huntsville: The Huntsville-Madison County Botanical Garden
6. Mobile: Mobile Botanical Gardens
7. Montgomery: Jasmine Hill Gardens
8. Theodore: Bellingrath Gardens

Birmingham

Arlington House and Garden
331 Cotton Avenue, SW
Birmingham, AL 35211

Tel. (205) 780-5656
Open: Tues.–Sat. 10–4; Sun. 1–4
Fee

The gardens of Arlington House are best visited in springtime, when the six acres are in colorful bloom. Arlington is Birmingham's last antebellum house in the beautiful Greek Revival style; it was enlarged from an 1820s dwelling in about 1850. It is noted for its six tapered square columns at the entrance portico. (The site has an appropriately intriguing story: late in the Civil War a female Confederate spy is believed to have hidden in the attic during the house's occupancy by the Union General James H. Wilson.) In fact, Arlington House's architecture and hillside setting with broad lawns and great oaks, boxwood, and old magnolias make it seem quintessentially Southern. The eight-room house (open to the public) is furnished with a nice collection of nineteenth-century American decorative arts and furniture.

The gardens are period pieces, which also evoke the antebellum era. Among the plantings are bright geraniums and coleuses, and from April to June you'll find many flowering magnolias, azaleas, dogwoods, and a lovely rose garden.

Birmingham Museum of Art,
  Charles W. Ireland Sculpture
  Garden
2000 8th Avenue North
Birmingham, AL 35203

Tel. (205) 254-2565
Open: Tues.–Sat. 10–5;
  Sun. noon–5
Free

This museum has both indoor and outdoor treasures. Its indoor collection includes Renaissance, Asian, and seventeenth- to nineteenth-century European and American art, pre-Columbian art and artifacts, and a large collection of Wedgwood china, as well as a particular focus on twentieth-century contemporary art. A recent addition is the multilevel outdoor sculpture garden which combines plantings and contemporary art.

Designed by a sculptor—an unusual occurrence—this garden is of interest both for its lovely landscape and its art. Elyn Zimmerman, a New York environmental sculptor, planned the garden, dividing it into three separate areas. The largest pieces of sculpture are on the upper plaza, which is gracefully laid out with a pergola covered with wisteria vines. Its centerpiece is a great waterfall sculpture by Zimmerman. There are other contemporary works by Sol Lewitt, Mel Chin, and George Sugarman. The plaza is picturesque, with its rushing water over granite blocks, curved garden wall, and great cypress trees.

On another level is Red Mountain terrace, which also involves water. Here, two rectangular pools designed by Valerie Jaudon are inlaid with colorful ceramic tiles in a mosaic pattern. Around the pools is a patio, itself surrounded by a delightful garden—particularly in springtime—when you'll find magnolias, dogwood, and azaleas abloom midst the sculpture.

The third section of the garden is sunken, and features a variety of temporary art installations. For those garden enthusiasts who enjoy seeing nature and art intermixed, this is an especially nice place to visit.

Birmingham Botanical Gardens   *Tel. (205) 879-1227*
2612 Lane Park Road   *Open: dawn to dusk*
Birmingham, AL 35223   *Free*

A botanical garden with 67 acres, this site is divided into twelve special areas—some outdoors and some in conservatories. Anyone with a special interest in Asian gardens will enjoy the Japanese garden (considered to be one of the finest in the country), with a bonsai garden, and a Zen garden. A traditional teahouse and lanterns in the Japanese garden were gifts from Japan.

Other major attractions are a rhododendron garden, a fern glade, and a rose garden (with some 2,000 bushes and 150 varieties). There are also a wildflower garden (created in what was once an old rock quarry), a magnolia garden, and gardens devoted to iris, and crape myrtle, among others. Special features here include a sensory garden with a touch-and-see nature trail, a giant floral clock, naturalized acres particularly for bird watching, and an area devoted to new ideas for southern home gardeners.

The greenhouses feature cacti and orchids, among their many displays and seasonal exhibitions. A camellia house with 125 varieties is a favorite. With numerous displays, educational events, and propagation houses open to the public, this is a garden that is truly inviting (year-round) to visitors with every kind of garden interest.

Gadsden

Noccalula Falls Botanical
Gardens
1500 Noccalula Road
(off Route 211)
Gadsden, AL 35902

Tel. (256) 543-7412
Open: daily 8 A.M. to sunset
Fee

These lovely 65 acres have a rare and beautiful site; they are along a rock gorge where the Black Creek River flows into a spectacular 90-foot waterfall. (Legend has it that it was named for an Indian chief's daughter, who jumped to her death over the falls because she was disappointed in love.) Though this is a major tourist site developed with a pioneer village and zoo, the gardens themselves include acres and acres of natural woodlands and trails and, of particular note, 25,000 azaleas—something to see when in bloom all at once. There are also giant evergreens, a picturesque covered bridge, flowerbeds—and a fine 10-acre botanical garden. There is also a 65-mile-long trail beginning here, that ends at another beautiful site of waterfalls: De Soto Falls Park in Fort Payne, as well as a 100-mile scenic drive from here on the Lookout Mountain Parkway to Chattanooga, Tennessee.

Huntsville

Huntsville-Madison County
Botanical Garden
4747 Bob Wallace Avenue
Huntsville, AL 35805

Tel. (256) 830-4447
Open: Mon.–Sat. 8–6:30;
Sun. 1–6:30
Fee

Though this is a small botanical garden, it has some interesting specialties: among them are a butterfly garden—a rare treat if you've never visited one. (A Butterfly House is soon to be added.) Also most unusual is a lunar greenhouse. There are also five acres of different types of gardens, including an aquatic garden, annuals, daylilies, ferns, herbs, and a variety of demonstration gardens. There are also nature trails and many educational programs. This is a recommended place to take the children for a look at many different aspects of natural life.

Mobile

Mobile Botanical Gardens
5151 Museum Drive
Mobile, AL 36608

Tel. (334) 342-0555
Open: daily 8–5
Free

This fairly new botanical garden is located in Municipal Park, with 64 lovely acres in the center of Mobile. Here you'll find a combination of gardens and woodland nature trails. Among the highlights are its collections of springtime blooms. Visit in late March through May to see exotic azaleas, rhododendrons, and magnolias in full glory. Also featured are several specialty gardens including an herb garden, a fragrance and texture garden for the blind, and camellias, hollies, and ferns. If you are in Mobile in springtime, don't miss the Azalea Trail Festival, a 35-mile driving tour that winds through the city, where azaleas are a specialty. (They were first introduced to Mobile early in the eighteenth century.) Information on the Festival is available by calling (334) 432-6162.

Montgomery

Jasmine Hill Gardens
3001 Jasmine Hill Road
Montgomery, AL 36106

Tel. (334) 567-6463
Open: Tues.–Sun. 9–5;
  Moon Strolls 6–10 P.M. Thurs.
  nearest full moon
Fee

This is a garden with a romantic bent. When there is a full moon you can actually stroll through this lovely spot at night, surrounded by flowering shrubs and Greek statuary, fountains, and reflecting pools. There is even a full-scale, exact replica of the ruins of the Temple of Hera in Olympia, Greece.

Even by daylight you'll find Jasmine Hill a treat. Open year-round, the 20 acres of gardens are a delight, mixing classical art with native stone walks, and extensive collections of blooming plants throughout. Of special note are the flowering cherry trees (visit in early spring), a collection of camellias, crape myrtles (visit in summer), and annuals throughout the year. There is a lily pond. And, of course, jasmines galore.

Jasmine Hill was developed in the 1920s by a couple named Fitzpatrick, who had a taste both for Greek and Roman antiquities and flowers. Among their treasures are reproductions of "The Dying Gaul," "Mourning Athena," "Marathon Boy," and some twenty additional pieces. Each sculpture is a focal point in its own setting, such as the goddess head that is reflected in the rectangular lily pond or the avenues of flowering cherries that frame mythical lions. In addition to walking through the gardens—by day or night—you can also visit the original 1830s settler's cottage on the estate (now a restaurant) and listen to concerts in an amphitheater.

Theodore

Bellingrath Gardens   *Tel. (334) 973-2217*
12401 Bellingrath Gardens Road   *Open: 8 A.M. to dusk*
Theodore, AL 36582   *Fee*

Twenty miles south of Mobile and one of the premier gardens in the region, this is a "don't miss" site for the garden tourist. Known as the "Charm Spot of the Deep South," these 65 acres of formal estate gardens are spectacular, with plantings designed to bloom each season of the year, so whenever you visit, you'll find it worthwhile.

Mr. and Mrs. Walter Bellingrath began the gardens in 1928 with a collection of azaleas planted around their fishing camp. Visits to European gardens encouraged them to create a small formal garden at the site. Since then, notable plantings have turned their vast estate into one of the showplaces of the South, with each month's display a spectacular event. (There is also a house to visit, filled with rare porcelains, silver, and antiques.)

The ongoing progression of blooms, for example, includes a springtime exhibit of hundreds of thousands of azaleas all flowering at once. (Visit in February and March.) Some of the plants are more than a century old. Similarly, an autumn display presents colorful chrysanthemums in vast array; there are some 60,000 plants with millions of blossoms! (This is, in fact, the largest chrysanthemum garden in the world.) There are seasonal displays—each more stunning than the last—of camellias (March), lilies (April), roses (planted in a great circular garden with its own daylily pools—abloom from spring through December), poinsettias, tulips, and a variety of other delights, including many exotic plantings, like the colorful, tropically lush cala-diums, dracaena, amaranthus, and dieffenbachia, which enjoy the hot Alabama summertime. Even August has its delights: African violets, salvias, orange ixora blossoms, brilliant oleander.

Set among great live-oak trees dripping with Spanish moss, the gardens include a great variety of venues, many suggested by garden styles around the world. Water is an important element in many of them. Among the attractions are an ecological Bayou Boardwalk (with views of all kinds of wildlife), conservatories of exotica, specialty gardens, a sunken garden with a loggia, a butterfly garden, a seasonally planted grotto, extraordinary rock gardens (where many of the African violets grow), formal parterres, an Oriental-American garden, a canal, marshes, a river, and even a lake. A winding brick path takes the visitor through the expansive grounds.

This is the kind of garden with its brilliant bursts of color, and magnificently large-scale, sweeping displays, that most of us can only dream about. (A Coca-Cola bottling fortune made it a reality.) Plan to spend a full day here (but remember, the gardens are extremely popular—visit on off-peak days, if possible).

FLORIDA

Coral Gables   Cypress Gardens

Daytona Area   Delray Beach

Fort Lauderdale Area   Fort Myers

Gainesville   Homestead

Jacksonville   Lake Wales

Marineland   Melbourne

Miami   Naples

Orlando   Ormond Beach

Palatka   Palm Beach

Point Washington   Saint Petersburg

Sarasota   Tallahassee

Tampa   Vero Beach

Walt Disney World   West Palm Beach

Winter Haven

1. Coral Gables: Fairchild Tropical Garden
2. Cypress Gardens: Florida Cypress Gardens
3. Daytona area: Sugar Mill Botanical Gardens
4. Delray Beach: Morikami Park
5. Fort Lauderdale area: Butterfly World
6. Fort Lauderdale area: Flamingo Gardens and Arboretum
7. Fort Myers: Edison-Ford Winter Estates
8. Gainesville: Kanapaha Botanical Gardens
9. Homestead: Coral Castle
10. Homestead: Everglades National Park
11. Homestead: Fruit and Spice Park
12. Homestead: Orchid Jungle
13. Jacksonville: Cummer Gallery of Art
14. Lake Wales: Bok Tower Gardens
15. Marineland: Washington Oaks State Gardens
16. Melbourne: Florida Institute of Technology Botanical Garden
17. Miami: Simpson Park Hammock
18. Miami: Vizcaya
19. Naples: Caribbean Gardens
20. Orlando: Harry P. Leu Gardens
21. Ormond Beach: Rockefeller Gardens
22. Palatka: Ravine State Gardens
23. Palm Beach: Cluett Memorial Garden
24. Palm Beach: Four Arts Garden
25. Point Washington: Eden State Gardens
26. Saint Petersburg: Sunken Gardens
27. Sarasota: Marie Selby Botanical Gardens
28. Sarasota: Ringling Museums and Gardens
29. Sarasota: Sarasota Jungle Gardens
30. Tallahassee: Alfred B. Maclay State Gardens
31. Tampa: Busch Gardens
32. Tampa: Eureka Springs Park
33. Vero Beach: McKee Botanical Garden
34. Walt Disney World
35. West Palm Beach: Mounts Botanical Garden
36. Winter Haven: Slocum Water Gardens

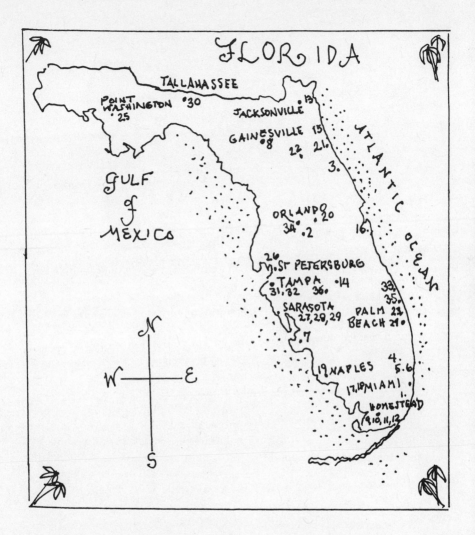

Coral Gables

Fairchild Tropical Garden
10901 Old Cutler Road
Miami, FL 33156

Tel. (305) 667-1651
Open: daily 9:30–4:30
Fee

This is a major garden of tropical plantings, encompassing some 83 acres. It is so large that you can take a tram around it, or you can walk through the noted palm and tropical flowering tree collection. There are lakes, shady areas, exotic plantings, and collections of tropical wonders, such as rare orchids and bromeliads. An unusually high overlook of 18 feet—in this very flat section of Florida—enables you to get a view from above.

Considered to be the largest tropical garden of its kind in the continental United States, Fairchild is a must-see stop for garden enthusiasts who are interested in tropical plantings. For this is not only a display garden but a living laboratory, a botanical garden for both tourists and scientists. It was the brainchild—in the 1930s—of Robert Montgomery, a lawyer and accountant with a love of plants, and David Fairchild, a botanist. The garden was designed for them by William Lyman Phillips. (His instructions noted that the place "should be a garden rather than a park," but there are nonetheless large open spaces, as well as the magnificent trees and shrubs.)

Plantings here are grouped according to botanical family. Each group of plantings is offset with open space—lawns or lakes. The designer conceived of the arrangement as a series of "openings"—from one section to the next, from large tranquil spaces to densely planted sections. Areas of the garden offer a great variety of shapes, textures, and colors; there is a Palm Glade (there are 700 species of palms at Fairchild), a rock garden, a rain forest, a rare plant house, a fern collection, many tropical flowering plants including bougainvillea, hibiscus, frangipani, ylang-ylang, and that plant with the wonderful name and daily changing colored blossoms: the Yesterday, Today, and Tomorrow shrub.

Cypress Gardens

Florida Cypress Gardens
2641 South Lake Summit Drive
Cypress Gardens, FL 33884

Tel. (800) 282-2123
Open: daily 9:30–5:30
Fee

This is a very large (200-acre) extravaganza, and one any garden enthusiast will want to visit. It is planted with spectacular tropical and native plants, and is a well-known tourist attraction. Founded (in what was once a swamp) in 1936 by a retired advertising executive named Richard Pope, it was designed specifically with beauty and attractiveness (and certainly some commercial interest) in mind. In fact, *Life* magazine once referred to it as a "photographer's paradise," and indeed, it has been used for movie sets and by numerous photographers, and visited by thousands and thousands of tourists. (Some say that Cypress Gardens is where Florida tourism began.) Though Mr. Pope was laughed at for choosing this site—he was known as "Swami of the Swamp" and "Maestro of the Muck"—his enterprise has become one of the most visited sites in the state. There are all of the usual tourist attractions too—and more, including a zoo, water skiing, ice skating exhibitions, and all kinds of events—both garden and non-garden related. Nonetheless, just as all of these visitors have found the gardens magnificent, so will you!

With one of the world's largest collections of tropical and subtropical plants in the world, Cypress Gardens offers vast areas of flowering beauty—and you needn't walk all through it. There are also canal boat tours, railroad tours, kiddie rides, and guided tours offered. Most notable is the Island in the Sky—a 16-story, 150-foot ride that soars above the park. There is a manmade Mediterranean waterfall (in this flat landscape!), and numerous fountains, walkways, formal gardens, and changing displays.

Theme gardens include a rose garden (with 500 species of roses), collections of orchids, gardenias, a forest garden, a butterfly garden (in a great Victorian glass house), vegetable and fruit gardens, a Biblical Garden (with some 25 species mentioned in the Bible), an Oriental garden, a French garden, educational exhibits, and no less than 8,000 different varieties of plantings from 90 different countries. Giant cypress trees—many with Spanish moss dripping from them—loom over delicate plants and pathways. Every plant is labeled, both in Latin and English.

There are numerous special garden events here too, each as flamboyant and extravagant as the next. For example, springtime brings extensive topiary displays (The Easter Bunny and a giant inch worm, among others), and a Victorian Garden Party event, in which creeping fig vine is used to create dozens and dozens of topiary figures. Forty thousand poinsettias decorate the grounds around Christmas time and in fall, the chrysanthemum blooms are said to number 2.5 million!

A visit here can be easily combined with the nearby Slocum Water Gardens in Winter Haven.

Daytona Area

Sugar Mill Botanical Gardens   *Tel. (904) 767-1735*
950 Old Sugar Mill Road   *Open: dawn to dusk*
Port Orange, FL 32125   *Free*

This fairly new 12-acre botanical garden may still be a work in progress, but it already boasts a variety of fine collections, as well as a natural area for hiking, (including an Ivy Lane and a Hammock Trail, a bog trail and an Audubon Trail). Built on the ruins of a mid-eighteenth-century English sugar mill that was destroyed in the Seminole Indian wars, it is a romantic combination of ruins and gardens. There are collections of camellias and magnolias, and a water garden. Daylilies and azaleas are also featured. There is a "Xeriscape" garden, devoted to plants that grow in very dry climates. You'll also find four stone dinosaurs guarding the pathways.

Delray Beach

Morikami Park   *Tel. (561) 499-0631*
4000 Morikami Park Road   *Open: Tues.–Sun. 10–5;*
Delray Beach, FL 33446   *closed holidays.*
                                    Free

For a change of pace from Florida's lush tropical gardens, you will enjoy this quiet Japanese museum and garden. Here you can learn about aspects of Japanese culture through permanent and changing exhibitions, and can wander through the serene one-mile guided nature trail and view a magnificent bonsai collection.

Morikami Gardens was founded by George Sukeji Morikami, who first came from Japan to Florida with a group of farmers in 1906. Though most of the colony disbanded, Morikami was able—at the age of 89 and after a long career in farming and real estate—to satisfy a lifelong desire to create a gift to the state of Florida. In 1976 he donated 200 acres to Palm Beach County, and had an authentic Japanese garden and museum constructed. Since the climates of Florida and Tokyo are so different, the planners adapted tropical plants from all over the world to the Japanese design.

But the clean raked sands, carefully-placed rocks, pools of koi fish, and gently running water are all thoroughly traditional to Japanese gardens, and above all, the peaceful stillness of the environment is typical of the great Eastern gardens. Bamboo walls enclose the bonsai collection. If you are not already aware of the Japanese garden ethos—with its unions of opposites, asymmetrical plantings, symbolic statuary, and reflective water—this garden will expand your knowledge and your enjoyment tremendously.

Fort Lauderdale Area

Butterfly World
Tradewinds Park
3600 W. Sample Road
Coconut Creek, FL 33073

Tel. (954) 977-4400.
Open: Mon.–Sat. 9–5; Sun. 1–5.
Fee

There are three acres of tropical gardens here, and the added attraction of thousands and thousands of colorful butterflies enjoying them. This is an intriguing spot, which includes a variety of different kinds of gardens: an English rose garden, a vine walk, a water garden, and a tropical rain forest. Also of note are an insectarium and nature walks. We recommend this outing for families with children, for here you will see not only attractive gardens but the interaction of insect life with the botanical—all in an attractive and fascinating environment.

Flamingo Gardens and
   Arboretum
3750 Flamingo Road
Davie, FL 33330

Tel. (954) 667-1651
Open: daily 9:30–4:30
Fee

This is as much a nature museum as a garden, with all kinds of natural life—from flamingos in their native habitat to rain forest, citrus grove, water fowl, and tropical flora and fauna of many different types. You can ride through the gardens and arboretum on a tram for more than a mile, viewing wildlife and growing things, including the world's largest collection of tropical butterflies called heliconias. In addition to seeing some 21 champion trees, you'll get a real taste of what a rain forest is really like. There is also an aviary and a museum devoted to the history of the Everglades.

Fort Myers

Edison-Ford Winter Estates
2350 McGregor Boulevard
Ft. Myers, FL 33901

Tel. (941) 334-7419.
Open: Mon.–Sat. 9–3:30;
 Sun. noon–3:30
Fee. Reservations required

Thomas Edison and Henry Ford made their winter homes next door to one another here in Ft. Myers. Each had a taste for gardens; today you can tour both estates together. You'll find Edison's riverfront estate (including his house and laboratory, now a museum) as well as a 14-acre botanical garden. (This is where he conducted botanical experiments as well as those for which he is so famous.)

You can walk among an impressive array of trees—many planted by the inventor himself—and see what is claimed to be the largest banyan tree in the country (though it was only two inches high when given to Edison). Other rare trees include a sloth tree from the West Indies, sapodillas, a sausage tree, a 100-foot hibiscus, and many more.

A visit includes a fascinating combination of history and botany and invention; you can even see an exhibit relating to the inventor's attempts to produce synthetic rubber from goldenrod.

Gainesville

Kanapaha Botanical Gardens
4700 SW 58th Drive
Gainesville, FL 32608

Tel. (352) 372-4981
Open: Mon., Tues., and Fri. 9–5;
 Wed., Sat., and Sun. 9 A.M.
 to dusk
Fee

Kanapaha Botanical Gardens, covering some 62 acres, is both a collection of eight specialty gardens and a great wildlife sanctuary, including original Indian trails, and walks taken by early American naturalist William Bartram. Rare trees and unusual carnivorous plants, bamboos, lotuses and other exotic species abound here, along with all kinds of Florida wildlife—from birds to alligators.

And what specialty gardens these are! Here you'll find gardens devoted to everything from bamboo to herbs, wildflowers to spectacular water lilies. Don't miss the special garden of hummingbirds, where a collection of flowers and plantings attract dozens of these tiny creatures. Or the Butterfly Garden, one of the best around, where masses of exquisite butterflies are fluttering about.

You'll also enjoy a Vinery with exotic vines from around the world growing on ornamental lattices, and a Sunken Garden (in a natural sinkhole) where ferns and palms and various unusual plants abound. There are also a Carnivorous Garden, a Water Garden, a Rock Garden, a Bog Garden, and the state's largest public Bamboo Garden. If you delight in lilies, come in August or September when the rarest bloom, but from February through the spring Kanapaha Gardens are awash in color as well.

Homestead

Coral Castle
28655 South Dixie Highway.
Homestead, FL 33030

Tel. (305) 248-6344
Open: daily 9–6
Fee

This fascinating sculpture/architecture site, situated within a walled compound is not the ordinary garden. It conjures up visions of an ancient Druid realm. Immense gates (one weighing nine tons!) reminiscent of Stonehenge open into a world created in the 1920s entirely by Edward Leedskalnin, a Latvian émigré. Built as a reclusive home for himself and a longed-for bride, it includes a two-story tower and curious outdoor garden rooms, all chiseled from coral rock. The rooms contain handmade stone furniture—beds, tables, love seats, a couch, and bathtub—as well as bold sculptures shaped like obelisks, moons, and stars.

The fiercely independent and eccentric owner conceived of this 10-acre site as his castle. Wishing to be independent of the outside world, he planted vegetables and fruit trees, flowering vines, shrubs, and flowers. These gardens, interspersed among the sculptures, feature species native to South Florida, as well as subtropical exotics.

Surprisingly, Leedskalnin welcomed occasional visitors to his private world. A bell is still located next to the front gate, instructing you to ring twice—no more, no less—as it did during his lifetime.

Everglades National Park	*Tel. (305) 247-6211*
U.S. Highway 1	*Open: daily, interpretative*
Homestead, FL 33030	*center 8–5*
	Fee

You can view this vast ecological spread by foot, boat, tram, or by car and you can rent both canoes and bikes here. This is a natural botanical garden, with typical Everglades bogs and plants and wildlife. There is a flamingo area (home also to pelicans and egrets), and some 345 different species of birds have been spotted here. Under the canopy of the hardwood forest there are also a hundred types of butterflies, some of them very rare. For those of us most interested in Everglades plant life, there is a pontoon service, which takes visitors into the heart of the swamp where wild flowers and tropical plants grow in profusion.

Fruit and Spice Park	*Tel. (305) 247-5727*
24801 SW 187th Avenue	*Open: daily 10–5*
Homestead, FL 33030	*Fee*

Instead of flowers, you'll discover an extraordinary collection of exotic fruits and spices, nuts, and herbs growing here—some 500 varieties from every corner of the world. This unique park, which covers 20 acres, was founded in 1944. An intriguing concept—you'll not only find it fascinating to look at, but you'll enjoy the wonderful exotic fragrances that fill the air. Visit this heady spot and bring a picnic (and purchase exotic fruits and nuts on the premises). Bring the children on this outing; they will be fascinated by seeing and tasting here.

Orchid Jungle	*Tel. (305) 247-4824*
U.S. Highway 1 at 272nd Street	*Open: daily 8:30–5:30*
Homestead, FL 33030	*Fee*

Orchid Jungle, which calls itself the world's largest orchid garden, in-

deed has 23 acres of natural forest here, with exotic plantings growing under the trees, and several greenhouses with additional rare orchids within. There is also a lath house with more orchids blooming.
Orchid Jungle is one of those rarities, a specialty garden that is devoted to only one type of plant in its myriad varieties. (If you think of
orchids merely as the lavender corsage sort, plan to visit here!)
Chances are you won't find a more comprehensive collection of orchids than this one. There is a special orchid show every day.

Jacksonville

Cummer Gallery of Art
829 Riverside Drive
Jacksonville, FL 32204

Tel. (904) 356-6857
Open: Tues.–Fri. 10–4; Sat. 12–5;
Sun. 2–5
Free

This two-and-a-half-acre garden surrounding a fine art museum was
begun almost a century ago at its charming site along the St. Johns
River. These are formal gardens replicating the Villa Gambreraia Garden in Italy. The Italianate and English style design features bulbs and
flowering shrubs and evergreens; best time for a visit to see the flowers and shrubs in bloom is spring. The Cummer Gallery art collection
features works from ancient Greece to modern times. But the gardens
are a period piece—a fine example of the formal gardens of the past.

Lake Wales

Bok Tower Gardens
11151 Tower Boulevard
Lake Wales, FL 33853

Tel. (941) 676-1408
Open: daily 8–5
Fee

Designed by the great landscape specialist Frederick Law Olmsted,
these gardens are special. Edward Bok, for whom they are named, was
a publisher and author from Holland who created this site for public
enjoyment in 1929. In his effort to beautify the landscape, he had a dramatic marble and coquina stone bell tower built and the gardens
planted around it. (You can hear one of the world's greatest carillons—
57 bells—played daily at every half hour, with a recital at 3 P.M.)
    The gardens are located at one of the highest points in the state of

Florida. When Olmsted undertook the design, the owner asked him to create a garden that would "touch the soul with beauty and quiet." The resulting landscape is filled with flowering trees and winding paths. The 128 acres are planted with camellias (November through March), magnolias, and azaleas (December through April), as well as a fine collection of palms. There is also a nature observatory overlooking a pond. This is a gentle and lovely place and there are many special events. Mr. Bok is known to have said, "Wherever your lives may be cast, make the world a bit better or more beautiful because you have lived in it." He took his own advice to heart.

Marineland

Washington Oaks State Gardens
State Route A1A
Marineland, FL

Tel. (904) 488-1234
Open: daily 8 A.M. to sunset
Fee

With the Atlantic Ocean and the Mantangas River just beside you, you can walk on a boardwalk and enjoy both the water vistas and the fine formal gardens in these state gardens in the north of Florida. An unusual combination of the formal and the natural, this site is particularly interesting. The 390 acres include all kinds of natural plants, rock formations, and a native hardwood hammock forest, as well as an abundant selection of azaleas, roses, camellias, and exotic species. This is a lovely spot and one that will capture the attention of both garden lovers and wanderers who prefer exploring the rocks and forest.

Melbourne

Florida Institute of Technology
Botanical Garden
150 West University Boulevard
Melbourne, FL 32901

Tel. (407) 768-8000, ext. 6123.
Open: daily, sunrise to sunset.
Free

If you are intrigued by palm trees, this is the place to visit. Over 2,000 palm trees of some 100 species grow in this 30-acre garden, which is adjacent to the landscaped Florida Tech campus. You'll also find a series of different habitats in this natural preserve, ranging from a lush grouping of hickories and oaks and other hardwoods, to sandy uplands with palmettos and pines. The Botanical Garden is a good place for a walk; you can traverse it on a mile-long trail with wooden bridges and paved paths.

Miami

Simpson Park Hammock
55 SW 17th Road
Miami
(mailing: 10110 SW 81st St.
Miami, FL 33173)

Tel. (305) 271-0735
Open: daily 10–5
Free

Surprisingly situated right in the heart of downtown Miami these eight and one half acres give us an idea of what the natural life of southern Florida looked like—a subtropical jungle. Here you'll see the native trees and plants of the area, along with resident wildlife that represent the area as it was about one hundred years ago. Today, the area is cared for—and provides a home for—many horticultural groups, including the local garden clubs that keep it going.

Vizcaya
Biscayne Bay
3251 S. Miami Avenue
Miami, FL 33131

Tel. (305) 250-9133
Open: daily 9:30–5, except
Christmas
Fee

This palatial waterside house and garden bring a touch of the Renaissance to South Florida. There is a 70-room Italian Renaissance palazzo with a great collection of objets d'art and furnishings from the first to the eighteenth centuries. And of special interest to us, you'll find a wonderful 12-acre subtropical garden based on Renaissance design.

Shaped like a giant fan spread out on a hillside, the garden is spectacular (and noted throughout the country as perhaps the finest Italianate garden in America), with its elegant architectural design, its fountains, parterres, pavilions, lagoons with islands, water displays, shell-lined grottoes, and sculpture—as well as its plantings. This is a place that takes the European idea of a formal garden to heart; it offers not just pretty flowers and trees, but a true sense of design and an elegant intermingling of art and nature. In the classical Renaissance style, the garden becomes an extension of the villa itself.

Villa Vizcaya, on the shore of Biscayne Bay, was designed to be the winter home of James Deering, of the International Harvester fortune, who settled in Miami for his health. Before building he traveled to Italy to survey the most beautiful gardens and palazzos. With the aid of Paul Chalfin, a painter and curator, he began collecting and planning for his own magnificent Italianate home and garden. Begun in 1914, the estate was built by a thousand artisans, many brought from Italy, under the guidance of a noted landscape architect, Diego Suarez. The garden took more than nine years to develop.

Like its Italian counterparts, it is primarily an evergreen garden, a haven of cool shade, reflective water, fountains, and antique art. Color here is used as an accent, rather than the rule. Where Italian plants would not thrive in the humid climate, all kinds of ingenious alternatives were developed. Thus, though the garden may seem to recreate a Mediterranean ambiance, it is actually filled with native plantings— displayed in thoroughly Italianate style. Though the fan-shaped formal gardens are the heart of Villa Vizcaya's design, there are gardens and art all around the property. Among the many treats here are the topiary shrubs and trees, the complex patterns of pathways and balustrades, the Maze Garden, the Theater Garden (which is a miniature version of a terraced ancient outdoor theater), the Secret Garden (complete with hidden grottoes), a Sensory Garden for the Blind, and the Fountain Garden, where there is an authentic seventeenth-century Italian fountain. Don't miss the domed garden house, called the "casino," the "peacock" bridge, and the marvelous collection of antique stone statuary throughout. On the shoreline is a U-shaped seawall, where an artistic Venetian-style stone barge landing accommodated the owner's gondola.

Some say that the best view of this unforgettable garden is from the second-floor windows or the terrace of the villa. But be sure to walk through its labyrinth of paths and pavilions anyway. You will not find another garden like it in this country.

Naples

Caribbean Gardens
1590 Goodlette Road
Naples, FL 33940

Tel. (941) 262-4053
Open: Tues.–Sun. 9–5
Fee

This tropical setting is home to both animals and plants. Parrots and other rare birds fly through the garden's 52 acres of jungle and plantings. There are stunning greenhouse collections of bromeliads and orchids, as well as great palms and dense groves of cypress. You can walk through the gardens or take a tram ride through the dense cypress groves and the acres of palm trees. This is a good outing for children, since, in addition to the many birds and jungle growth, there are also a zoo and animal shows.

Orlando

Harry P. Leu Gardens
1920 North Forest Avenue
Orlando, FL 32803

Tel. (407) 246-2620
Open: winter, 9–5; spring–fall,
Mon.–Sat. 9–8; Sun. 9–6
Fee

Camellias are a specialty in this large, lush 56-acre garden in the heart of the historic district of Orlando and on the shore of Lake Rowena. Botanical collections feature all kinds of tropical plants and palms, as well as a rose collection covering a full acre. In fact, there are over 2,000 different varieties of plants here. Created in 1936, the garden has had a long time to mature, and it is a delightful place to wander along boardwalks, footbridges and pathways, amid many gazebos and fountains. If you need a respite from the nearby Disney hoopla, visit these lovely acres.

Harry P. Leu's extraordinary collection of camellias has a serendipitous history. He was searching for a profitable crop to grow on his oak-shaded lands. On travels in India and Tibet he and his wife were fascinated by a shade-loving camellia whose leaves were a rare ingredient in the finest British teas. He decided to import the plant for his own acres, and it did indeed prosper. But the camellia turned out to be the wrong species for tea—though it had a magnificent Asian blossom much like a rose. Leu gave up the idea of tea, and instead created these beautiful camellia gardens, ordering dozens of additional species of the Asian plants. Leu gave the gardens to the city of Orlando in 1961; it has been a major attraction ever since.

In addition to the great collection of 2,000 camellias, Florida's largest, you'll find a number of floral displays, including a giant clock made of flowers, a lily circle, and many areas devoted to specific plantings: an azalea area, a ravine garden (which features birds of paradise, bananas, flowering vines, and ferns), and a conservatory with orchids and other tropical plants. Other specialties include ginger and impatiens and flowers native to the area. To see the camellias at their best, visit from October through March.

You can also visit a restored historic house from the late 1800s.

Ormond Beach

Rockefeller Gardens
25 Riverside Drive
Ormond Beach, FL 32074

Tel. (904) 673-4701
Open: daily
Free

Here you'll find an authentic restoration of a two-acre garden on the Halifax River front that belonged to John D. Rockefeller, Sr. in the early 1900s. There are citrus trees, a grand promenade, and a generally attractive air to these gardens, with streams and small bridges, and a variety of seasonal flower displays during the year. The Rockefeller mansion, called The Casements, across the river, is open for tours. (Not far away, you'll find the Ormond War Memorial Art Galleries and Gardens. On a four-acre site, this semi-tropical park features stands of native bamboo, flowering trees and shrubs, and many water plants.)

Palatka

Ravine State Gardens
1600 Twigg Street
Palatka, FL 32178

Tel. (904) 329-3721
Open: daily, dawn to dusk
Free

You can either drive or walk through these 85 acres of subtropical gardens. Beautifully set in a natural ravine and surrounding landscape of blooming shrubs and flowers, the gardens are partly formal, partly natural. Natural species are favored. Azaleas are the featured attraction from January to April, with more than 100,000 of them (some 50 varieties) abloom then.

Formed by water flowing through the sandy west shore of the St. John's River, the ravine became covered with indigenous shrubs, pines, magnolias, dogwoods, and many other species of trees. In the 1930s the park was established, and plantings of azaleas and camellias were added to complement the flowering dogwoods and other spring-time shrubs. There are also a water lily pond, and terrific hikes. Tours are offered during azalea season.

Palm Beach

Cluett Memorial Garden
  Church of Bethesda-by-the-Sea,
  South County Road and
  Barton Avenue
Palm Beach, FL 33480

Tel. (561) 655-4554
Open: daily 9–5
Fee

It is always a special treat to find a hidden garden. Palm Beach actually has two of them. To reach this surprisingly large, formal, tropical garden you enter through the east arcade of a 1925 Gothic church. Privately maintained by the Cluett family, this extensive garden features many exotic plantings and changing flower displays; it is ornamented with pergolas, pools, and fountains. For a quiet and lovely oasis in the heart of Palm Beach, make a stop here.

Four Arts Garden
Four Arts Plaza
Royal Palm Way
Palm Beach, FL 33480

Tel. (561) 655-7226
Open: Mon.–Sat. 10–5; Sun. 2–5
Fee

Although it encompasses only one acre tucked behind the Four Arts Library in Palm Beach, this is a showcase garden. Originally created in 1938 by the Palm Beach Garden Club to demonstrate what plants could be grown in the hot, humid, hurricane-prone climate, it soon developed into an unusually well landscaped and attractive spot. A terrific collection of demonstration gardens is maintained here. Although each of the seven sections is not large, their variety and charm are well known throughout the area.

Among the specialties are: a Jungle Garden (featuring tropical plants such as bromeliads, prayer plants, and palms), a Rose Garden, (which blooms year-round), a British Colonial Garden (with clipped hedges and symmetrical patterns), a crescent-shaped Moonlight Garden (much of which has white flowers that bloom—and have a heady fragrance at night—as in the seventeenth-century gardens of the Indian moguls), a Spanish Garden (with traditional wishing well and tile design), and a Tropical Fruit Garden. There are also small examples of an herb garden in a neat brick-lined area, and a small, enclosed Madonna Garden with a stephanotis-covered fountain. Each of these special sections flows into the next in seamless arrangement.

Of particular interest is a walled Chinese Garden. It is entered through a Moon-gate, and has its own symbolic, antique statuary, Asian plants, and a small pond with moss-covered stones, as well as traditional Chinese arrangement. Here, the ladies of the Garden Club have been able to replace certain Asian plants with American equivalents, which still maintain the ambiance and significance of the traditional Chinese garden. This is a thoughtfully designed and carefully maintained example of a centuries-old tradition.

Point Washington

Eden State Gardens
181 Eden Garden Road
Point Washington, FL 32454

Tel. (850) 231-4214
Open: daily 8 A.M. to sunset
Fee

Now part of the Florida park system, Eden State Gardens is the former home of William Henry Wesley, a lumber baron who lived here a century ago. There is a restored Greek Revival mansion (which you can tour for a taste of turn-of-the-century Gold Coast life), and a fine 11-acre garden featuring azaleas, camellias, and great oak trees dotting the lawns. Visit in March for the best of the spectacular azalea display, or from October through May for camellias galore; you'll enjoy the moss-draped live oaks year-round.

Saint Petersburg

Sunken Gardens
1825 Fourth Street North
St. Petersburg, FL 33704

Tel. (727) 896-3186
Open: daily 9 A.M. to sunset
Fee

Any exotic plant aficionado won't want to miss the many tropical plants found in this eight-acre garden, which include 50,000 varieties of subtropical plants set in each year, and a rare collection of orchids—more than 1,000 examples. The variety here is enormous—

from colorful vines to rare African violets to bromeliads and ferns. There is also an aviary with tropical birds—peacocks and parrots— and a jungle section devoted to other animals. (There are also a variety of touristy attractions—including alligator wrestling—and a large number of visitors. Try to visit in off-peak times.)

Sarasota

Marie Selby Botanical Gardens   *Tel. (941) 366-5731*
811 South Palm Avenue   *Open: daily 10–5*
Sarasota, FL 34236   *Fee*

Orchids and bromeliads are the specialty here. There are 6,000 of them. Any orchid enthusiast should make this a must-see site. The delicate colors and fragrance make this a rare experience. (They range from the most endangered of species to the more familiar.) But there is much more to see. In the 11-acre garden there are also some 20 different theme gardens and seven greenhouses. The collection has over 20,000 plants—an extraordinary number for any garden.

Many of the plants were collected in the wild, and there are exotic plants as well as more common varieties. In fact, many of the botanical species here were collected in far away places, such as Brazil, Borneo, Ecuador, Indonesia, and Costa Rica.

Among the theme gardens are a butterfly garden, a great favorite, a bamboo pavilion, a waterfall garden, palm and banyan groves, a succulent garden, water lilies, and a spectacular hibiscus garden. Also featured in the lush environment are oddities like carnivorous pitcher plants, malabar spinach from Sri Lanka, vegetable sponge from Africa, and the world's largest collection of African violets. There are tropical edibles like papayas and cassava and figs and pineapples. With its location along Sarasota Bay, the garden offers a Baywalk Sanctuary with an elevated boardwalk that wanders through a mangrove swamp. In the Tropical Display House there are myriad lush plantings, many of which dangle above you from a 10-foot tall volcanic rock wall.

Another unusual feature is the collection of epiphytes (or plants that feed on air and moisture) and grow on 12 ancient oaks. A visit here will truly give you a sense of the tropical jungle—not just of the artificial amusement park variety, but of the real botanical type—an experience not to be missed.

Ringling Museums and Gardens   *Tel. (941) 355-5101*
U.S. 41   *Open: daily 10–6; Thurs. until 10*
Sarasota, FL 33578   *Fee*

Here you'll see the noted Ringling Museum of Art, a mansion patterned after the Doge's palace in Venice, and a delightful Circus Museum, the restored 1798 Italian Asolo Theater (offering many performances), as well as 38 acres of plantings. For the garden enthusiast, a visit here will include the sumptuous 350-foot museum court garden—an elegant combination of plantings and statuary and fountains—a formal rose garden, a parterre garden, and a "secret garden." The gardens here are part of a large and impressive complex representing aspects of all of the arts.

Sarasota Jungle Gardens   *Tel. (941) 355-5305*
3701 Bayshore Road   *Open: daily 9–5*
Sarasota, FL 34234   *Fee*

Sarasota's oldest tourist attraction, the Jungle Gardens are formally arranged with lush garden trails. These winding brick paths take you through an untamed landscape. In contrast, once you get to the gardens you'll be able to enjoy thousands of different plants, as well as birds both wild and tame, among them pink flamingos and cockatoos. Major horticultural attractions include gardenias, bougainvilleas, hibiscus, banana groves, fern gardens, and traditional palms. There is plenty to amuse the family here. Shows of tropical birds, trained by prisoners in a California jail, are a popular attraction. There is also a collection of some 3,000 shells here, and a display of many jungle reptiles.

Tallahassee

Alfred B. Maclay State Gardens   *Tel. (850) 487-4115*
3540 Thomasville Road   *Open: daily 9–5*
Tallahassee, FL 32308   *Fee*

This beautiful 300-acre site is a former private estate, now a state park. There are formal gardens, flowering trees (including dogwood, magnolia and cherry), and demonstration gardens. The Maclays began creating their extensive garden in 1923, and over the years it has matured into a lovely spot, particularly in winter and early spring (when the Maclays were in residence).

Twenty-eight acres of the extensive estate are landscaped, some of them around a large picturesque lake. Though Maclay favored azaleas and particularly camellias, he also planted many exotic species. There are also familiar blooms like pansies, daylilies, and irises. This is thought to be one of the South's most extensive collection of azaleas and camellias (to see these specialties in bloom, visit in March). There is an architectural feel to many of these gardens; there are archways, walkways, circular flowerbeds, and such attractions as a Camellia Walk, a Walled Garden (which surrounds a courtyard with a small pool), and Lake Vista, which has a reflecting pool bordered by white azaleas, palms, and cypress trees.

Tampa

Busch Gardens
3000 Busch Boulevard
Tampa, FL 33612

Tel. (813) 977-6606
Open: daily 9:30–6
Fee

If you like bustling environments with things to do, see, and buy, then don't miss these famous gardens. Included in the 300-acre park are flowers, tropical trees and shrubs, as well as a good-sized zoo, bird and dolphin shows, sky-ride, monorail, restaurant, and brewery tour. Eight different theme sections evoke the spirit of turn-of-the-century Africa, here called "The Dark Continent." Among the thematic exhibits are sections devoted to Nairobi and baby animals, Morocco and a North African ambiance, the Serengeti Plain and its native wildlife, and the Bird Gardens and Aviary with over 2,000 specimens. There are seasonal and tropical plantings throughout this entertainment complex.

Eureka Springs Park
6400 Eureka Springs Road
Tampa, FL 33610

Tel. (813) 626-7994
Open: daily 8–6
Free

Thirty-one acres are devoted to a botanical garden of rare and unusual plants, all of them native to Florida. In addition to conservatories featuring orchids and other tropical plants, there are extensive outdoor gardens with walkways ornamented by trellises. There are interpretive trails and a variety of appealing walks. Less well-known than its neighbor, Busch Gardens, this park is a serious botanical garden for those with a taste for horticultural and aesthetic pleasures.

Vero Beach

McKee Botanical Garden
350 U.S. Highway 1
Vero Beach, FL 32962

Tel. (561) 794-0601
Open: daily 10–5
Fee

One of the oldest botanical gardens in the state and an early tourist attraction, McKee Botanical Garden was developed in 1932. It quickly became known for its beautiful orchids and water lily collections, as well as for its hybridizing of exotic plants. Now a major project of the Indian River Land Trust, the Garden has been named to the National Register of Historic Places. It has undergone extensive renovation in the last few years. If water lilies and exotic plants are your interest, this is an attraction you won't want to miss.

Walt Disney World

Walt Disney World Resort
   and Epcot
Interstate 4 and Florida 535
Lake Buena Vista, FL 32830

Tel. (407) 824-4321
   (horticultural information)
Open: daily; hours vary
   seasonally
Fee

While you may not have come to these popular sites primarily to see gardens, you will be delighted to discover the scope of horticultural pleasures here. This 30,500-acre site has enough flowers and trees and other plantings to interest anyone with a taste for horticultural beauty. Indeed, the size and number of flower gardens is dazzling: over three million bedding plants are displayed in some 300,000 square feet of flower gardens each year. And there are topiary and theme gardens, trees from some 50 countries, as well as the United States, and a nature preserve. The landscape is strategically planted to add character, color, mood, and backdrop to one of the world's busiest stages. (An overall picture of the size and scope of the horticultural efforts here is suggested by the fact that it requires no less than 630 people to see to the landscape.)

In addition to the carefully landscaped grounds throughout (like the palm-lined boulevard at the Disney-MGM Studios), certain areas are specially devoted to garden pleasures. As you organize your time here, plan to see the major garden areas.

Most formal and elegant are Le Notre Gardens in the France Showcase at Epcot, where Baroque-style French gardens have been recreated in all their splendor—including a "*parterre de broderie*" (a garden laid out in embroidery patterns). Also at Epcot there is a six-acre agricultural showcase, which includes a boatride through greenhouses and experimental growing areas. The largest bedding area at Epcot covers 20,000 square feet and is planted with seasonal blooms year round; this vast flowerbed contains up to 20,000 plantings. Another spot to see at Epcot is the topiary garden of specially pruned trees in geometric shapes at Journey into Imagination. The gardens at Epcot are showcased for six weeks each spring at their International Flower and Garden Festival.

A must-see site for garden lovers is the rose garden at Cinderella Castle in the Magic Kingdom Park. Here there are 40 different varieties of roses—some 13,000 plants. The rose garden is abloom all year round. And while at Disney's Animal Kingdom, a visitor interested in jungle plantings will find the landscape filled with exotic species.

The horticultural ambiance here ranges from the very civilized to the wild—from the carefully maintained 200 whimsical topiary shapes (including Disney characters) and thousands of hanging flower baskets, to the 11,000-acre Walt Disney Wilderness Preserve, which is devoted to the restoration and preservation of an adjacent wilderness. Opened to the public in 1995, this preserve protects native species of flora and fauna at the headwaters of the Kissimmee River.

West Palm Beach

Mounts Botanical Garden
531 North Military Trail
West Palm Beach, FL 33415

Tel. (561) 233-1749
Open: Mon.–Sat. 8:30–4:30;
Sun. 10–5
Free

A variety of gardens here include citrus and tropical fruit trees, a Fern House, a Lily Pond, a Touch Garden, and gardens devoted to hibiscus, roses, and herbs. This 13-acre site also has an unusual menu of programs and educational events dealing with such subjects as salt-tolerant plants and native species; its horticultural programs are one of its major objectives.

But even if you just come to see the pretty growing things, you will find plenty to interest you.

Winter Haven

Slocum Water Gardens
1101 Cypress Gardens Road
Winter Haven, FL 33880

Tel. (863) 299-1896
Open: Mon.–Fri. 8–4; Sat. 8–12
Free

This delightful seven-and-a-half-acre water garden includes ponds, fountains, goldfish, and aquatic plants. But the real specialty here is water lilies—100 varieties of them. These acres of water gardens are truly a fascinating sight; if you've never visited an extensive water garden, you will be delighted by the sight as you walk the paths above the water. You can also purchase and bring home some of the water lilies with you from the garden. This is one of the rare retail establishments included in this book; it is well worth visiting, whether you choose to buy plants or just wander about.

GEORGIA

Adairsville   Athens
Atlanta   Augusta
Decatur   Fort Valley
Hiawassee   Loganville
Lookout Mountain   Metter
Milledgeville   Mount Berry
Pine Mountain   Savannah
Waycross

1. Adairsville: Barnsley Gardens
2. Athens: Founders Memorial Garden
3. Athens: State Botanical Garden of Georgia
4. Atlanta: Atlanta Botanical Garden
5. Atlanta: Cator Woolford Memorial Garden
6. Atlanta: The Gardens of H.M. Patterson & Sons
7. Atlanta: Robert L. Staton Rose Garden
8. Atlanta: Atlanta History Center
9. Augusta: Riverwalk
10. Decatur: Georgia Perimeter College Botanical Garden
11. Fort Valley: Massee Lane Gardens
12. Hiawassee: Fred Hamilton Rhododendron Garden
13. Loganville: Vines Botanical Gardens
14. Lookout Mountain: Rock City Gardens
15. Metter: Guido Gardens
16. Milledgeville: Lockerly Arboretum
17. Mount Berry: Oak Hill at the Martha Berry Museum
18. Pine Mountain: Callaway Gardens
19. Savannah: Chatham County Garden Center and Botanical Gardens
20. Savannah: Forsyth Park
21. Savannah: Richardson-Owens-Thomas House and Gardens
22. Waycross: Okefenokee Swamp Park

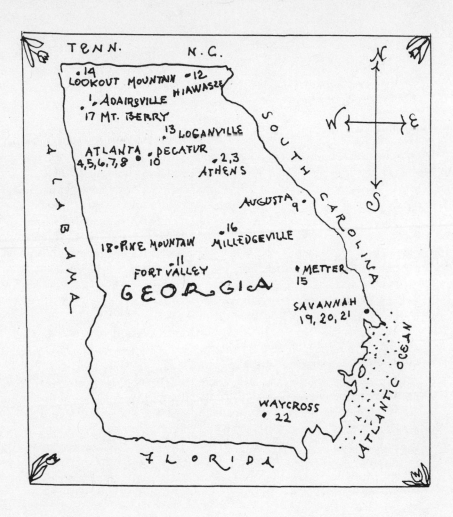

Adairsville

Barnsley Gardens
597 Barnsley Gardens Road
Adairsville, GA 30103

Tel. (770) 773-7480
Open: March–Nov.,
   Sat.–Sun. 11 A.M. to dusk
Fee

These beguiling gardens in the rolling northwest Georgia mountains combine the romantic ruins of an Italianate villa with 30 acres of landscaped grounds and flower gardens. Once the much larger country estate of Godfrey Barnsley, an Englishman who came to Georgia in the nineteenth century to seek his fortune in cotton, it has had a long and rich history, one also tinged with tragedy. (It was the scene of a family murder in the 1930s.) In 1841, Barnsley built this rather extravagant estate, which he called Woodlands—for his wife, Julia, and their growing family. An avid amateur botanist and gardener, it appears that he based his landscape designs on the published manuals of Andrew Jackson Downing, the most renowned landscape architect of the time. With its many exotic plants from around the world, as well as native rhododendrons and azaleas (literally hundreds), Woodlands was a real showplace. So much so that, during the Civil War, General McPherson and his troops were careful not to damage it.

Unfortunately, during the late nineteenth century, the property suffered from lack of care; on top of everything else, a vicious tornado left the manor house without a roof in 1906. The sad deterioration of Woodlands was reversed in the 1970s, when Prince Hubertus Fugger of Germany bought the estate. It has since undergone extensive restoration. The romantic ruins of the main house have been reclaimed from a jungle of wisteria vines and preserved, as have other historic structures on the property, and the once-fabled gardens are being brought back to life.

The haunted-looking brick mansion is now the picturesque setting for a semi-outdoor art gallery and museum documenting the history of the site. You will want to walk around its arched passageways and explore it, as well as the surrounding gardens, fields, and woods.

Among the garden's many pleasures are a boxwood parterre with Renaissance-style fountain, a rose garden, broad lawns with herbaceous borders, rock and bog gardens, a group of ponds surrounded by ornamental grasses and other plantings, a wildflower meadow, and a rhododendron hill. You are free to explore on your own or take a guided tour conducted by a horticulturist or historian, depending on your interests.

Athens

Founders Memorial Garden
The Garden Club of Georgia, Inc.
State Headquarters House
325 South Lumpkin Street
Athens, GA 30602-1865

Tel. (706) 542-3631
Open: daily dawn to dusk
Free

Created as a living tribute to the 12 Georgia ladies who in 1891 formed the first garden club in the nation (there are now almost 10,000 such organizations), this is a gracious two-and-a-half-acre garden on the leafy grounds of the University of Georgia campus. It was conceived in the early 1940s by Hubert Owens, head of the University's Department of Landscape Architecture, not only to honor the founders, but also to provide an outdoor laboratory of regional ornamental plants for both students and visitors.

Existing historic buildings—a picturesque 1857 historic Greek Revival house (now headquarters for the Garden Club of Georgia), a small kitchen building and smokehouse—became the backdrops for the elegant garden. Featured are graceful, connected garden rooms, including a formal boxwood parterre, a perennial garden, a courtyard of paving stones arranged in circles, terraces overlooking the landscape, a camellia walk and arbor, and a more freeform, shaded garden with azaleas, rhododendrons, ground covers, and stone paths.

One of the favorite areas within the beautifully maintained site is the colonial boxwood garden. Surrounded by a white picket fence, it combines dwarf evergreen hedges trimmed in circular motifs, brick walkways, and beds of native peach, Cherokee rose, and cotton boll. Beside it, a small terrace flows into the perennial, or serpentine, garden, so called because of its undulating brick wall surrounding a broad lawn and collection of annuals and perennials. Nearby is the outstanding camellia collection (dedicated to Owens) and arboretum of mature trees. Throughout the garden you will find some of the best examples of Georgia and Piedmont species in the South, including double flowering dogwood, magnolia, leatherleaf viburnum, and flowering quince.

A fitting memorial to those dedicated garden lovers of the past century, the garden is a serene oasis that invites contemplation and careful study, or a leisurely stroll in a historic setting.

State Botanical Garden   *Tel. (706) 542-1244*
   of Georgia   *Open: daily 8 A.M. to dusk*
2450 South Milledge Avenue   *Free*
Athens, GA 30605

Aptly describing itself as "a living laboratory," this 313-acre botanical garden of the University of Georgia is dedicated to the study and enjoyment of plants and nature. With its specialty gardens, miles of winding woodland trails (color-coded, for easy identification), and pristine, modern conservatory, it provides the ideal setting for a nice, long garden walk.

Its 11 theme gardens (with several more in the planning stage) include many seen in other botanic sites: a Shade Garden, Dahlia Garden, Ground Cover Collection, Trial Garden, Native Flora Garden, Rose Garden, and Annual/Perennial Garden, among others. But more unusual and especially inviting is the International Garden. (You can enjoy a nice view of it from the airy tearoom in the Visitor Center.) Here, alongside a stream and over an arched, flower-filled stone bridge, a sequence of horticultural collections flow gracefully into one another, portraying the important historic connections between people and plants and the evolution of botanical gardens. These beautiful and enlightening exhibits feature plants from the Middle East and the Mediterranean, Spanish America, the American South, and the Orient; herb collections used for dye, fragrance, ceremonial, and culinary purposes; examples of threatened and endangered species and thoughts on conservation; and displays honoring historic personages, such as John Bartram, whose tireless efforts in plant gathering have significantly furthered the study of botany.

The gardens on these vast grounds (all well marked and clearly identified) connect via gently sloping paths, many shaded with laurel, magnolia, dogwood, viburnum, azaleas, rhododendrons, and other native species. The Conservatory contains fine collections of orchids, tropical food, beverage, and spice crops, and exotic palms.

For an unexpected pleasure after seeing the gardens, stop at the Day Chapel, a 1994 soaring structure made of cypress and glass, peacefully set in thick woods beyond the gardens.

Atlanta

Atlanta Botanical Garden
1345 Piedmont Avenue
Atlanta, GA 30309

Tel. (404) 876-5859
Open: Tues.–Sun. 9–6
Fee

A lavender wisteria vine covering a wood trellis graces the entrance of this delightful 30-acre urban oasis, located at the northern end of Atlanta's Piedmont Park. Within lies a world of spectacular flowering trees and blossoms, from pink and white dogwood, to cherries, azaleas, and crab apples. Springtime features masses of wildflowers, tulips, hyacinths, pansies, and iris. An All-America Rose Selections Garden (not surprisingly, the setting for many weddings) adds elegance and charm. You will also find a rock garden, an herb and knot garden, a vegetable garden, and a very pleasant woodland trail with native shrubs.

But the centerpiece of the Botanical Garden is without doubt its dazzling Conservatory. Opened in 1989, the Dorothy Chapman Fuqua Conservatory encloses some 16,000 square feet into tropical and desert climatic zones. More than 6,000 plants flourish in this house of glass, many of which are rare or endangered. In the desert environment is a rich collection of succulents. Under the massive tropical rotunda (which is 50 feet tall and visible throughout the garden) a dramatic 14-foot cascade tumbles over volcanic lava, surrounded by exotic orchids, ferns, and very high Madagascar palm trees. Brightly colored parrots fly around freely to the sounds of frogs (these "poison-arrow" frogs come from the rain forest in South America and are nearly extinct). You could well imagine yourself in a real jungle!

The Garden also has collections of carnivorous plants. In fact, just outside the conservatory is a bog featuring some of these curiosities, including Venus flytraps. Children will enjoy this site and will be fascinated by the displays.

The Atlanta Botanical Garden is a very pleasant place to visit, whether you are here to get ideas for your own garden or simply to enjoy its natural beauties.

Cator Woolford Memorial Garden
1815 Ponce de Leon Avenue, NW
Atlanta, GA 30307

Tel. (404) 377-3836
Open: daily, dawn to dusk
Free

This secluded garden, nestled in historic Druid Hills, a leafy Atlanta enclave designed over a century ago by the prolific Frederick Law Olmsted, is a serene oasis of flowers, columns, grassy areas, and woods. Once part of the 33-acre estate of entrepreneur Cator Woolford, it was originally a private garden, restored and redesigned in the 1920s by a prominent Philadelphia landscape architect. When the property was sold to the Children's Rehabilitation Center in the 1940s, it became a therapeutic garden to enhance the nature experiences of the disabled. In the past few years it has been a favorite site for outdoor weddings and other social events—not surprisingly, in view of its romantic setting.

The centerpiece of the six-acre garden is a broad lawn surrounded with colorful plantings, including pansies, iris, peonies, phlox, azaleas, old-fashioned roses, and decorative grasses, as well as a graceful colonnade. Winding paths lead to a rock garden, wildflower glen, and bog garden, along a little stream flanked with bamboo. The pretty woodland walkways, within a deep virgin forest, are dotted with dogwoods, azaleas, and other native shrubs. Many of the garden structures—stone benches, archways, and columns—add a touch of old world charm.

The Gardens of H.M. Patterson
* & Sons*
Spring Hill
1020 Spring Street, NW
Atlanta, GA 30309

and
Oglethorpe Hill
4550 Peachtree Road, NE
Atlanta, GA 30319
Tel. (404) 876-1022
Open: daylight hours
Free

A walk in a garden surrounding a funeral home might not strike most people as an especially inviting proposition, but a visit to either of these two similar sites might revise this view. The gardens at Spring Hill, situated on a busy midtown street corner, are the earlier of the two. Conceived in the late 1920s by architect Philip Shutze to complement his elegant design for the house, the gardens at Spring Hill (and their mirror image at Oglethorpe Hill) are divided into two sections, one formal, the other less so. On the north end of the building is the intimate, partially enclosed formal area, with symmetrical rows of boxwoods, geometric flowerbeds, and grassy cutouts. A graceful female statue and a small fountain with a basin of aquatic plants add classical touches. Spring Hill's south garden features a gently sloping hillside of colorful flowers and shrubs amid rocks and stone pathways.

Spring Hill and Oglethorpe Hill have been managed by the same Patterson family since the beginning, and the gardens, with minor exceptions, have shown the same continuity over the decades, in terms of design and plantings.

Robert L. Staton Rose Garden	*Tel. (404) 378-4311*
Fernbank Museum of Natural	*Open: daily, sunrise to sunset*
* History*	*Free*
156 Heaton Park Drive, NE	
Atlanta, GA 30307	

This one-acre delight of fragrance and color is a must for any rose fancier. Here you can find just about every type of rose you have ever heard of, from miniatures, to hybrids, to climbing roses. There are altogether about 1,300 plants representing some 250 varieties, all coming from three sources: All American Rose Selection test plants, American Rose Society Award of Excellence Miniature test plants, and donated named roses. Some are in tidy rows of rectangular beds outlined in brick, while others climb gracefully onto wooden trellises. Most flowers are labeled, except for those undergoing a period of evaluation to determine their suitability for the local climate.

The rose garden bears the name of its founder, a precocious rosarian who joined the American Rose Society while still in his teens. Later, while working for the Fernbank Science Center, he came up with the idea for the garden.

Because of Atlanta's long growing season, the rose garden is in bloom from early May well into fall, until the first frost.

Atlanta History Center	*Tel. (404) 814-4000*
130 West Paces Ferry Road, NW	*Open: Mon.–Sat. 10–5:30;*
Atlanta, GA 30305	* Sun. noon–5:30; closed*
	* holidays*
	Fee

The Atlanta History Center, situated on what was once a private estate with surrounding woods, chronicles the natural and historic evolution of the region through a collection of indoor and outdoor exhibits. There is much to see on these spacious grounds in addition to the museum and library, and you should allow time to savor it all, from reconstructed nineteenth-century Georgia farm buildings, to many delightful gardens and winding woodland trails. The centerpiece of the site is the Swan House and its lovely, enclosed boxwood garden. This classic-style mansion, designed by Philip Shutze in the late 1920s for the prominent Inman family, contains furnishings and artifacts reflecting the glamour of that era.

The formal Italianate garden features a boxwood parterre, which has recently been meticulously restored to its original splendor, a gracious central fountain basin, elegant columns, urns, potted hydrangeas, grassy borders, gravel paths, and carefully arranged plantings. Perennial beds, just recreated after extensive research on plants that might have been there originally, are now filled with peonies, iris, phlox, hosta, and candytuft. It's difficult to imagine that this quiet and peaceful garden is in the middle of a very lively city.

Among the other garden offerings at the Center are an Asian-American Garden, complete with stylish gazebo and Japanese maples, exotic azaleas, and hydrangeas; an enticing, shaded garden on the site of an abandoned quarry, enhanced by a stream, waterfall, and granite outcrops; a rhododendron garden with flowering native shrubs and trees; a group of charming nineteenth-century-style flower, herb, and vegetable gardens outside the rustic farm buildings; and the newest of all, the Gardens for Peace.

The latter, an intimate, circular forest garden within the Swan Woods Trail, offers ferns, rhododendrons, evergreens, wildflowers, and small stone benches for rest and contemplation. Featured at one end is a bronze sculpture called "The Peace Tree," depicting five life-size figures clasping hands around a tree. This garden is the first of a network of international gardens symbolizing peace (others are presently located in Tbilisi and in Madrid) whose purpose is to promote world peace and respect for the environment.

You can also enjoy a stroll through the half-mile Swan Woods Trail. Referred to as an "outdoor laboratory," it wanders past azaleas, tulip poplars, magnolias, and other woodland species of the Georgia Piedmont, and is dotted with little signs describing in some detail the ecosystem of the region.

Augusta

Riverwalk
Augusta/Richmond Country
  Convention
and Visitors Bureau
P.O. Box 1331
Augusta, GA 30903

Tel. (706) 823-6600
Open: daily, dawn to dusk
Free

Since 1987 Augusta has been blessed with a most picturesque garden walk along its Savannah riverfront. During the 1980s, when city leaders around the country began to understand the commercial and aesthetic value in revitalizing their downtowns, the idea of creating walkways to take advantage of the spectacular river scenery was conceived.

The riverwalk is along two promenades, about five city blocks in length. One, built on top of a levee dating from the early 1900s, commands striking views of both city and river; the other, just above the riverbank, affords a closer look at the water.

The beautifully landscaped promenades are endowed with dogwoods, azaleas, river birch trees, and other varieties native to the region. A Japanese Garden—that might come as somewhat of a surprise in this kind of setting—is also included on the grounds, as are picnic tables, park benches, playground, and dock. You will find the combination of riverviews and garden pleasures irresistible.

Decatur

Georgia Perimeter College
  Botanical Garden
3251 Panthersville Road
Decatur, GA 30034

Tel. (404) 244-5052
Open: daily, dawn to dusk
Free

In the suburban town of Decatur, just east of Atlanta, you'll find this little botanical garden, tucked away behind the modern buildings of a local college and a high school. At first glance you might think of it as a quite modest garden; that is, until you realize how ambitious it actually is.

Begun in 1990 by the students of the college (then named De Kalb College), its mission has been to preserve and propagate native plant species. Through the dedication and hard work of individuals and local organizations, the site (also known as the Wildflower Center of Georgia) is presently the state's largest all-native garden. And it is still expanding. Eventually, some 2,000 species will be represented here.

The grounds feature rare, hard-to-grow, sometimes endangered species situated on four acres within a flood plain. In the front of the botanic garden are raised, contained beds of sun-loving flowers, shrubs, and small trees. There are more than can be enumerated, bearing such names as hairy sumac, white beard tongue, blazing star, streamside wild indigo, Barbara's button, and blanket flower. Behind, in a woodland with a creek, are the shade varieties. You can walk along a nature trail and view ferns, iris, black cohosh, azaleas, needle palm, orchids, Jack in the pulpit, and Carolina phlox, to cite only a few.

Everything is carefully labeled throughout the garden. Indeed, if it weren't for the fact that this is, after all, an educational facility, you might wish to see fewer of these somewhat distracting, little white markings. But you can learn a great deal here and enjoy the garden at the same time.

Fort Valley

Massee Lane Gardens
One Massee Lane
Fort Valley, GA 31030

Tel. (912) 967-2358
Open: Dec.–March, Mon.–Sat.
9–5; Sun. 1–5. April–Nov.,
Mon.–Fri. 9–4
Fee

The centerpiece of this 10-acre garden in the heart of Georgia is the camellia. The site, surrounded by a landscape of peach and pecan trees, boasts one of the largest camellia collections (over 1,000 varieties) anywhere in the world and is, in fact, the headquarters of the American Camellia Society.

In 1936, when a severe storm devastated what was then land dedicated to growing peach trees for commercial use, the owner, Dave Strother, began cultivating camellias. His passion for this glorious, colorful blossom became such that he eventually founded the American Camellia Society. In 1965 he donated his farm acreage and collection to the Society.

The camellia, an ancient flower first appreciated by the Chinese some 4,000 years ago, is one of those rarities that blooms during the winter months. When most other flowers lie dormant, it shines in brilliant pinks, reds, and whites. The time to visit these gardens is between November and April, with a peak during February and early March.

The Massee Lane Gardens offer other garden pleasures besides the camellia, however. There are smaller gardens featuring roses, perennials, daylilies, and even an enclosed Japanese garden. Also on the grounds are a camellia greenhouse, an extensive library (with rich collections on camellias), a museum, and a gallery displaying porcelain birds.

Hiawassee

Fred Hamilton Rhododendron   *Tel. (706) 896-4191*
Garden   *Open: daily, dawn to dusk*
P.O. Box 444   *Free*
Hiawassee, GA 30546

As its name indicates, this garden celebrates the glorious rhododendron—and in an enthusiastic way. On these 17 acres in Northern Georgia, quite close to the North Carolina border, some 2,000 rhododendron plants, representing 400 varieties, are on display. From spring to early fall, rhododendron lovers from all over congregate at this site—the state's largest such specialty garden—some for its annual Rhododendron Festival in mid-May.

The creation of Fred and Hazel Hamilton, the garden was at first a private spot, about three miles from its present site. When the Hamiltons donated it to the Georgia Mountain State Fair in 1982, its numerous plants were moved to where it is now, near Lake Chatuge. Since that time, more and more plants have been added, with more to come.

In addition to the featured rhododendrons, you'll find azaleas, dogwoods, tulip magnolias, and quite a number of wildflower varieties. The blooming peak is from the last week of April to early June, so plan accordingly.

Loganville

Vines Botanical Gardens
3500 Oak Grove Road
Loganville, GA 30249

Tel. (770) 466-7532
Open: April–Oct., Tues.–Sun.
10–7; Nov.–March,
Tues.–Sun. 10–5
Free

Vines Botanical Gardens, one of the newer gardens in the region, is also one of its most idyllic. On 25 immaculate acres outside a small town just east of Atlanta, it features a landscape of colorful plantings set around a picturesque lake complete with bridge, fountains, swans, and geese. Beyond are a group of charming gardens, some graced with antique statuary and yet more fountains, others set along streams and ponds.

During its short history the site has undergone several incarnations, from being the private estate of Charles and Myrna Adams in the mid-1980s, to becoming a public garden in 1990; later it was taken over by the Vines Botanical Gardens Foundation (named after Mrs. Adams' father, Odie Vines), and was yet again privatized—with guaranteed public access.

Among the garden pleasures are: the Asian Garden, a peaceful tableau of iris, azaleas, rhododendrons, and Japanese maples along a pond and stream; the White Garden, with a white gazebo framing all-white blossoms; the Rose Colonnade Garden, featuring four statues representing the seasons, classic columns with wisterias, and a profusion of antique roses; Pappy's Garden, a colorful collection of old-fashioned flowers on a gentle slope; and the Brook Garden, including a rock-lined stream and terraced garden of shrubs and perennials.

Connecting the gardens are intertwining paths and boardwalks, stone steps, little bridges, and wooden pavilions. The elegant manor house, set high on the hill with spectacular views of the lake and gardens, is now home to various amenities, including a popular restaurant.

Lookout Mountain

Rock City Gardens
Off Highway 85, just south
of the Tennessee border

Tel. (706) 820-2531
Open: daily, except Christmas,
8:30 to dusk
Fee

Rock City Gardens is a craggy landscape of paths and steps and narrow bridges winding among huge rocks and ravines high on a mountain. You walk on self-guided trails, alongside hundreds of species of wildflowers, shrubs, and other plants native to this mountain region. Those with a sense of adventure, agile enough to negotiate challenging places (with such names as "Fat Man's Squeeze," "Needle's Eye," and "Balanced Rock"), are also rewarded with a glorious view encompassing seven states.

Actually, Rock City Gardens is part of Lookout Mountain, a favorite tourist destination just outside of Chattanooga, extending into Georgia and even Alabama (our walk is technically in Georgia, with access from Tennessee). Rock City became an attraction during the lean Depression years, when the entrepreneurial Garnet and Frieda Carter decided to charge admission to their most unusual 10-acre property on top of Lookout Mountain. To publicize their "Rock City Gardens" they hired people to paint "See Rock City" on hundreds of barn roofs along major highways all over, from the Gulf Coast to the Great Lakes.

After this unconventional "gardenwalk," you might stop at the nearby Lookout Mountain Natural Bridge, a natural rock arch, where groups of Spiritualists used to conduct seances and other ceremonies. This quiet, uncommercial spot is a pleasant place for a picnic.

Metter

Guido Gardens
600 North Lewis Street
Route 121 North
Metter, GA 30439

Tel. (912) 685-2222
Open: dawn to dusk
Free

This pretty, three-acre oasis of fountains, brooks, waterfalls, and bright blossoms is more than a your standard pleasure garden. Indeed, it is the setting for television and radio broadcasts that are heard by some 30 million people worldwide. For many years, Dr. and Mrs. Guido have preached their simple, nondenominational evangelical message from this site, which was donated to them 25 years ago by the local mayor so they could pursue their ministry.

The well-kept garden features native Georgia plantings—dogwoods, pines, and many, many azaleas. Other highlights include a water garden complete with rocks, exotic koi fish and lily pads, a picturesque gazebo, and a chapel in a peaceful pine grove. There are benches for quiet meditation and even soft, background music for additional inspiration. Visitors are also invited to take a guided tour of the adjacent Sower Studio, production home of the broadcasts.

Milledgeville

Lockerly Arboretum
1534 Irwinton Road

Milledgeville, GA 31061

Tel. (912) 452-2112
Open: Mon.–Fri. 8:30–4:30; Sat. 1–5
Free

Lockerly Arboretum is a living laboratory dedicated to the conservation, beautification, and study of plants. On 47 acres right in the middle of the state, you can examine more than 6,000 species, from native azaleas, hostas, rhododendrons, camellias, and grasses, to exotic tropical or desert plants.

The best way to see this untouristy site is by foot, along well-marked and maintained trails, taking along with you a detailed map which is available at the office. (You can also drive to most displays.) Among the arboretum's many offerings is a sand tracking bed (with animal footprints); a vineyard; an aquatic garden; a berry bramble; specialty beds with herbs, iris, lilies, and perennials; a young forest; a butterfly garden; and two greenhouses and a museum.

The Arboretum was the creation of Edward J. Grassman, a New Jersey nature and ornithology enthusiast, whose mission was to educate students of all ages, encouraging them to share their botanic knowledge with others.

Mount Berry

Oak Hill at the Martha Berry
  Museum
189 Mount Berry Station
Mount Berry, GA 30149

Tel. (706) 291-1883
Open: Tues.–Sat. 10–5; Sun. 1–5; closed on major holidays
Fee

The 170-acre gardens at Oak Hill, among Georgia's oldest and most venerable, will appeal to both nature and history devotees. Situated near Rome, in an agricultural region rich with limestone, they surround a gracious antebellum plantation house, one of the few in Georgia that survived the Civil War unscathed. There is a great deal to see at this site: the gardens themselves, the manor, a museum, and a vast and impressive college campus right next door.

The grounds near the house are exquisitely landscaped with formal gardens; beyond are rolling parklands with meadows, ponds, and nature trails. The oldest remaining garden at Oak Hill, the Formal Garden, was begun by Frances Berry in the early years of the Civil War. Her daughter, Martha, added the enchanting Sunken Garden many years later. But Martha's interests were primarily educational, rather than botanical; indeed, the tiny log cabin school she built on her inherited land to educate local children was the nucleus for Berry College, now a 30,000-acre campus adjacent to Oak Hill's mansion and gardens. You might also be interested in seeing the Original Cabin dating from 1873, known as the "birthplace of Berry College," as well as the college itself, best seen by driving through its extensive campus.

Before actually visiting the gardens you might like to take a quick tour of the museum and mansion, which will give you an interesting overview of Martha Berry, her family, and the evolution of the property. (The recently renovated Martha Berry Museum sets the stage, with exhibits on her life; there are also paintings from the family collection by Thomas Sully and others.)

The gardens were opened to the public in 1972. Among their many delights is Frances Berry's Formal Boxwood Garden, with its gracious flagstone walkways outlined in boxwood and flowerbeds, fountain pool, and adjoining rose garden. Paths lead to the nearby Goldfish Garden (a favorite of Martha's), complete with pond, traditional knot garden, and outer beds of annuals and perennials. The picturesque Sunken Garden, also called the Terrace Garden, features a charming stone fountain surrounded by flowering cherry trees given to Martha by the emperor of Japan in the early 1930s; beneath them are thousands of daylilies that are in full bloom in early April and then again in July. Other garden highlights include the Sundial Garden (annuals and perennials); three greenhouses containing over 25,000 plants; hillside nature trails, with daffodils and other native plants; the wildflower meadow; and the All-America Selection Display Garden (one of only five in the state).

Pine Mountain

Callaway Gardens
P.O. Box 2000
Pine Mountain, GA 31822-2000

Tel. (800) Callaway (225-5292)
Open: May–Sept., daily 7–7;
  check hours during other
  months
Fee

Callaway Gardens, one of the premier family resorts and gardens in the country, is a vast, 2,500-acre site in the rolling Appalachian foothills. Here, on ancient territory known as Pine Mountain (some geologists claim it is America's oldest land, described as the worn-down tailbone of the Appalachians), people of all ages can find relaxation, inspiration, and an appreciation of the natural world. Among Callaway's many offerings are 13 miles of scenic drives, bicycle trails, woodland walking trails rich with wildflowers, acres of garden conservatories and flowerbeds, and a large fruit and vegetable garden. (There are even golf courses, a 175-acre lake stocked for fishing, a large manmade beach, and tennis courts.) And Callaway also boasts one of the most magnificent azalea collections anywhere, thousands upon thousands of them, representing some 750 varieties.

The creators of this extraordinary place were Cason and Virginia Callaway who, in the 1930s, acquired a large tract of land that had been worn down by generations of cotton cropping. Originally meant as their private family retreat, the property evolved into a much more ambitious project, as they bought more and more land, restored forests, formed lakes, built trails through the woods, and created "gardens prettier than anything since the Garden of Eden." Opened to the public in 1952, the site was dedicated to enhance people's appreciation of nature through its many horticultural and educational displays and activities.

There are many garden pleasures to be found at Callaway. The John A. Sibley Horticultural Center (opened in 1984), among the most advanced greenhouse-garden complexes anywhere, includes five acres of indoor and outdoor displays. Its conservatory features exotic collections, as well major floral themes that are continually changed according to season. The outdoor gardens not only include lawns graced with old-fashioned flowerbeds and mixed borders, but sometimes—much to the delight of children—plants shaped into fanciful creatures, such as peacocks and even dinosaurs.

Children will also love the Cecil B. Day Butterfly Center, with its rich collections of tropical plants and butterflies contained within a spectacular 7,000-square-foot, octagonal glass space. Just outside the conservatory are small butterfly gardens, showing visitors which plants to cultivate in order to attract these species.

The seven-and-a-half-acre Mr. Cason's Vegetable Garden (now providing much of the several restaurants' delicious produce) was planned as a demonstration garden, since Callaway and his wife felt that people should be given the opportunity to observe the growing of fruits and vegetables.

Visitors can enjoy walking, biking, or birding along the Azalea Trail, the Laurel Springs Trail, Rhododendron Trail, Holly Trail, Wildflower Trail, and Mountain Creek Trail. Note that you can rent bicycles and electric cars to tour the gardens, which are also accessible by car, tram, an on foot.

Savannah

*Chatham County Garden Center
and Botanical Gardens
1388 Eisenhower Drive
Savannah, GA 31406*

*Tel. (912) 355-3883
Open: Gardens, daily, from
dawn to dusk; Center,
Mon.–Fri. 10–2
Free*

It comes as a surprise to learn that these charming gardens are on land once used as a prison farm. In 1991 the property was given to a nonprofit organization, to be developed into gardens and an educational center. A historic 1840s wooden farm house about to be demolished was transported to these premises to serve as the garden center headquarters.

Since its official opening in 1997, the 10-acre site has served to educate the public in conservation, horticulture, landscape design, even garden therapy. Courses and lectures are routinely given in botany and related fields; tours of these and other botanical gardens are conducted; and the already fine collection of native trees (some quite mature), shrubs, and flowers is being enlarged.

An army of dedicated volunteers serves to maintain impeccably the various gardens: the Azalea and Camellia Garden, the Native Plant Garden, the Kitchen Garden, the Herb Parterre, the Four Seasons Garden, the Rose Garden, the Shade Garden, and the Children's Garden, among others. The property also includes a picturesque pond, an inviting forest with nature trails, meadows filled with wildflowers, and even an ongoing archaeological dig where students can be seen busy at work.

Bear in mind that, although you are free to walk around the gardens on your own at any time, you can only visit the restored old farmhouse during the week, when the Center is open.

Forsyth Park	*Tel. (912) 651-6610*
(South of Gaston, between	*Open: daily, dawn to dusk*
Whitaker and Drayton Streets)	*Free*
Park and Tree Commission	
P.O. Box 1027	
Savannah, GA 31402	

Savannah is not only celebrated for its charming historic houses but also for its delightful "squares," that string of intimate, jewel-like commons, some of which have graced the city for well over 200 years. These rectangular, impeccably maintained oases, 24 in all, contain the inevitable oaks (yes, dripping with Spanish moss), azaleas and other blossoms, and fountains and monuments.

Forsyth Park, sometimes referred to as the "Last Square" because of its location, is also the city's largest park. Encompassing 21 acres, it includes parkland with gardens and a magnificent central fountain. This 1858 cast-iron fountain, a replica of one in Cuzco, Peru, has recently been restored and is a favorite Savannah landmark.

The gardens are a colorful collection of azaleas, magnolias, and palmettos punctuating the atmospheric oak trees. Completing the beautifully tended gardens is a Fragrance Garden for the Blind, with many differently textured plants.

The Richardson-Owens-Thomas	*Tel. (912) 233-9743*
House and Gardens	*Open: Tues.–Sat. 10–5;*
124 Abercorn Street	*Sun.–Mon. 2–5; closed*
Savannah, GA 31401	*January and major holidays*
	Fee

This elegant house with its enclosed garden stands out among Savannah's historic sites. Considered to be one of the best examples of English Regency architecture in the country, the stylish house was designed by a young English architect named William Jay (one of the first professionally trained architects practicing in the United States) and built between 1816 and 1819. After its original owner, Richard Richardson, suffered financial losses, it became an elegant boarding house (where the Marquis de Lafayette stayed and delivered a speech in 1825), then was purchased by the Owens family. In 1951 the house was bequeathed (by Margaret Thomas, the Owens' granddaughter) to the Telfair Academy of Arts and Sciences for use as a museum.

The intimate (1/8-acre), walled garden is an English-style parterre, with a small central fountain, stone walkways, and flowerbeds bordered with short, clipped boxwoods. Here you will see varieties of azaleas, nandinas, junipers, old-fashioned roses, and mock oranges, among other plants compatible with the temperate Savannah climate. Although not added until the 1950s, the garden has the feeling of one dating from the early 1800s. Installed in what used to be the stable yard of the house, it is surrounded with walls now mostly covered with vines.

The house (which can be visited only by guided tour) has an outstanding collection of decorative arts, including fine furniture, paintings, porcelains, and locally made textiles. You can walk around the garden on your own, savoring its peaceful and charming aura.

Waycross

Okefenokee Swamp Park
U.S. Highway 1 and Route 23
Waycross, GA 31501

Tel. (912) 283-0583
Open: June–Aug., daily 9–6:30;
Sept.–May, daily 9–5:30
Fee

A remarkable adventure awaits you, one that will take you deep into what has been called "America's greatest natural botanical garden." The Okefenokee Swamp Park, a National Wildlife Refuge located within nearly a half million acres of wetlands in southeastern Georgia, is richly endowed with unusual plants and animals.

This vast, jungly wilderness of forests, islands, and lily-filled waterways surrounded by great stands of overhanging live oaks and towering cypress can be visited on foot via walking trails and boardwalks, by small railway, or—for those who wish to explore the deeper reaches of the swamp—by boat. (Boat tours of all kinds are available.)

The park offers interpretive exhibits, wildlife shows, and lectures. To view the displays are a lagoon amphitheater, living swamp observatory, nature center, animal habitats, and a 90-foot observation tower. Anyone who has a spirit of adventure and is intrigued by rare flora or fauna—and does not mind the few tourist trappings that inevitably surround such a site—will find this a memorable experience.

KENTUCKY

Clermont

Harrodsburg

Irvington

Lexington

Louisville

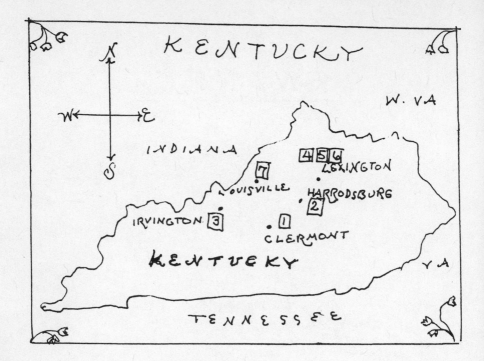

1. Clermont: Bernheim Arboretum and Research Forest
2. Harrodsburg: Shaker Village of Pleasant Hill
3. Irvington: Broadmoor Garden and Conservatory
4. Lexington: Ashland
5. Lexington: Lexington Cemetery
6. Lexington: University of Kentucky Arboretum
7. Louisville: Nature Center and Beargrass Creek State Nature Preserve

Clermont

Bernheim Arboretum and
Research Forest
Highway 245
Clermont, KY 40110

Tel. (502) 955-8512
Open: Mon.–Sat. 9–5; Sun., 12–4
Free (except weekends)

It's hard to imagine that an over-exploited farmland once occupied this site. In the late 1920s Isaac Bernheim, a young, conservation-minded German immigrant living in Louisville, gave this 10,000-acre tract to the state for the creation of a nature sanctuary. Over the years it has evolved into a rich forest, combined with wide open meadows and a beautifully maintained arboretum.

Much of the deep and extensive wilderness is kept as a research forest for state universities and colleges, and it is an ideal refuge for a rich variety of birds and other animal species. The public part of Bernheim includes some 35 miles of hiking trails amidst woodlands and the parklike arboretum.

This is an unusually well tended arboretum. Its 250 acres contain almost 2,000 carefully labeled plants. A scenic road takes you past stretches of meadows, ornamental gardens, and ponds—where you will likely see hundreds of waterfowl. Self-guided trails loop through wooded areas and fields, amid flowering trees and shrubs (azaleas, rhododendrons, dogwoods, crab apples), lush grasses, and wildflowers. Among the arboretum's special offerings are its highly regarded holly collection (one of the best in the country), as well as its ginkgoes, oaks, and horsechestnuts. A Nature Center provides exhibits of flora and wildlife, as well as workshops and classes.

Harrodsburg

Shaker Village of Pleasant Hill
3501 Lexington Road
Harrodsburg, KY 40330

Tel. (606) 734-5411
Open: daily 10–4:30
Fee

Set amid 2,700 acres of bluegrass farmland lies this restored Shaker village of some 30 original buildings. Although not technically a garden, this popular historic site does include small medicinal and herb gardens, in keeping with the Shaker tradition. One visits Shaker Village for the total experience, gardens included.

The Shakers, a nineteenth-century American utopian sect, believed in living a quiet and peaceful life apart from the rest of a world they viewed as disorderly and decadent; their communities were isolated and self-sufficient. In addition to making the graceful, simple furniture and other functional crafts they are so well known for, they cultivated vegetable and herb gardens for their own use. These tended to be small and intimate, and always tidy and pleasing to the eye.

You can take a self-guided tour through the buildings, as well as the gardens (these are, of course, best seen during the summer months). You will see working studios featuring weaving, furniture making, and candlemaking, among other crafts. The village was built on an unusually picturesque stretch of the Kentucky River, which the Shakers used for commerce with the outside world. As part of your tour you can enjoy a delightful hourlong river excursion on the stern-wheeler *Dixie Belle*, available several times daily.

Irvington

Broadmoor Garden
and Conservatory
Box 387/Hwy. 60 East
Irvington, KY 40146

Tel. (502) 547-4200
Open: Fri.–Sun. noon to 6
Fee

This 400-acre site offers many a garden pleasure, from extensive water gardens with pools, fountains, and waterfalls, to a tropical plant conservatory, to miles of wildflower gardens. There are rose gardens, iris-lily gardens, and garden statuary, adding a European flavor to this Kentucky landscape.

It is, in fact, largely in Europe that the creators of Broadmoor found their inspiration. While visiting the Kukenhoff Gardens in Holland (among other famous garden sites in Europe) during the mid-1980s, Mary Ann Tobin and Brucie Beard decided to build their own public garden on a 2,400-acre farm just 50 miles southwest of Louisville. In keeping with the farmlike ambiance (and perhaps with children in mind) they added quite a variety of animals—swans, peacocks, guinea hens, and pigmy goats—as well as some delightful animal topiaries.

But Broadmoor is not just for children. Any and all visitors—from sometime gardeners to professional horticulturists to families on a picnic outing—are bound to enjoy this lovely spot.

Lexington

Ashland
120 Sycamore Road
Lexington, KY 40502

Tel. (606) 266-8581
Open: daily, dawn to dusk
Fee

Ashland, one of Lexington's most appealing destinations, combines a gracious historic house with formal gardens. Once the estate of the illustrious statesman Henry Clay ("The Great Compromiser") and his wife Lucretia, it is now a museum containing nineteenth-century family memorabilia surrounded by 20 acres of gardens and woodlands. And what lovely grounds these are!

The Clays, both great garden lovers, wanted a grand landscape to complement their elegant mansion (designed in part by Pierre L'Enfant, the brilliant architect/designer of Washington, DC). In their heyday, in the early to mid-1800s, these gardens were vast, encompassing some 600 acres that even included orchards, along with parterres and other planted areas.

The present garden is much smaller, but still retains the spirit and style of the original. Lovingly tended by the Garden Club of Lexington, it features geometric flowerbeds, brick walls covered with ivy, carefully clipped boxwood hedges, and many, many old-fashioned blossoms. Depending on when you visit, you'll find roses, daylilies, geraniums, dahlias, and a wonderful collection of peonies.

If you stroll beyond the formal area you'll discover some unusual trees, including a gingko (Clay actually brought this species to Kentucky), and such nineteenth-century outbuildings as two round icehouses, smokehouses, and carriage houses.

You can explore Ashland on your own, although guided tours are available.

Lexington Cemetery
833 W. Main Street
Lexington, KY 40508

Tel. (606) 255-5522
Open: daily 8–5
Free

Although our most beautiful cemeteries tend to be carefully planted and well cared for, they are not necessarily places for a garden walk. Lexington Cemetery is one of the exceptions, offering a spectacular arboretum and two formal garden areas, along with many historic monuments.

The cemetery dates back to 1849, a time when the idea of the public park was taking hold across the country. In that spirit, it was conceived not only as a burial site but also as a peaceful spot for families to spend some leisurely moments.

Amid these 170 bucolic acres are some 200 varieties of trees, including an ancient linden tree, weeping cherries, ginkgoes, southern magnolias, panicle hydrangeas, and many evergreens. The three-acre garden area has a delightful sunken garden and colorful displays of bulbs, roses, iris, and lilies, among other flowers. Adding to the quiet and dignified aura are the unusual memorials (Henry Clay was among those buried here), some adorned with striking statuary.

A stroll in this lovely spot is sure to please those who love gardens and nature, as well as history.

University of Kentucky Arboretum *Tel. (606) 257-9339*
Alumni Drive *Open: dawn to dusk*
Lexington, KY 40508 *Free*

Though relatively young (1991), this lovely arboretum is remarkably well established. The fact that it is still evolving makes it also an interesting place to visit for those who like to see the process of creating a landscape.

Since 1996 more than 1,500 flowering shrubs and trees have been planted, and more are being added. As you walk about in this peaceful setting which is somewhat removed from the bustling campus, you can enjoy a variety of demonstration gardens (including "idea gardens" to inspire amateur—as well as professional—gardeners), an herb and knot garden, a Shakespearean garden, and even fountains. There are plans for a children's garden, a small amphitheater, and additional waterworks.

A two-mile trail called a "Walk Across Kentucky" is being developed; it will feature native plants from the state's seven geophysical areas. Beyond it is a bluegrass woodland, where you are welcome to continue your nature exploration.

The Arboretum has an ambitious program of special events throughout the year. In addition to lecture series and seasonal displays, there are art exhibits, band concerts, stargazing, apple tastings, a Shakespearean festival, and winter nature walks.

Louisville

Louisville Nature Center and
 Beargrass Creek State
 Nature Preserve
3745 Illinois Avenue
Louisville, KY 40213

Tel. (502) 458-1328
Open: daily 8:30–4:30; Sat. 10–2
Free

Located in the heart of the city, the Nature Center and adjacent Preserve offer a forest habitat rich with many varieties of animal and plant life.

While the Center is the educational facility for promoting the study of nature (it features programs for children and adults, lectures, hands-on demonstrations, and many inviting excursions), the Preserve is the actual "laboratory" for this work. Here, within some 41 acres of second growth forest, you can see over 180 species of trees and flowering shrubs, as well as hundreds of birds. (Bird watching is a favorite activity here.) Springtime brings masses of delicate wildflowers, with guided walks for those so inclined.

LOUISIANA

Avery Island

Loranger

Many

New Iberia

New Orleans

St. Francisville

Shreveport

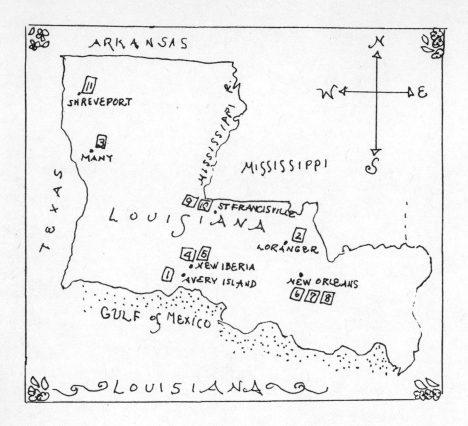

1. Avery Island: Jungle Gardens
2. Loranger: Zemurray Gardens
3. Many: Hodges Gardens
4. New Iberia: Live Oaks Gardens
   (Rip Van Winkle Gardens)
5. New Iberia: Shadows-on-the-
   Teche
6. New Orleans: Longue Vue
   Gardens
7. New Orleans: New Orleans
   Botanical Garden
8. New Orleans: Ursuline Convent
9. St. Francisville: Afton Villa
10. St. Francisville: Rosedown
    Plantation and Gardens
11. Shreveport: The Gardens of the
    American Rose Center

Avery Island

Jungle Gardens
Highway 329
Avery Island, LA 70513

Tel. (318) 369-6243
Open: daily 9–5, except holidays
Fee

True to its name, Jungle Gardens is a lush habitat for exotic plants and animals in a naturalistic environment. Within its 200 acres are groves of palms and bamboo and live oaks, swamplands and lagoons with crocodiles cruising about lazily, and thousands of snowy egrets and herons. But the site is more than a haven for the exotic, offering in fact an eclectic collection of tropical, subtropical, and temperate species from around the world.

On this salt dome hill, just after the Civil War, the McIlhenny family cultivated rows of hot red peppers for making tabasco sauce, their sensational new invention. (You can still see thousands of these colorful plants and visit the nearby tabasco factory.) It was not until some years later that Edward McIlhenny, family heir and amateur naturalist, introduced to his garden hundreds of unusual plants and animals from his worldwide travels. He apparently liked the idea of mixing rare with native plants, and Jungle Gardens, an imaginative combination of these, was launched.

Today's gardens include lotus and papyrus from the Nile, iris from Siberia, bamboo from China, as well as thousands of camellias (one of the best collections in Louisiana), azaleas, magnolias, and other local favorites. Among the garden's special viewing treats are the thousands of egrets that have thrived here thanks to Edward McIlhenny's efforts to save this once endangered species. Visitors enjoy watching the graceful white birds as they fly over marshlands in search of food.

The gardens are served by seven miles of winding drives and walking paths that lead to various points of interest, with some surprises along the way. Among these is the not-to-be-missed Chinese pagoda (housing an authentic eleventh-century Buddha) perched high atop a stone cairn. Enjoy a fine view of it from the bayou, while surrounded by ducks, geese, and swans.

Loranger

Zemurray Gardens
23115 Zemurray Gardens Drive
Loranger, LA 70446

Tel. (504) 878-2284
Open: March to mid-April, 10–6
    (call to confirm exact dates)
Fee

This is a private garden open to the public only during a six-week period in early spring, when its masses of azaleas and camellias come magically to life. Located within a 150-acre woodland, it sits picturesquely along the shores of a serene lake.

When the Zemurray family bought this remarkable property in the late 1920s, they dammed a stream and spillway to form the 20-acre lake (aptly called Mirror Lake). And because they were fond of spring blossoms, especially azaleas—of which there are now more than 250,000—they planted what have become profuse collections of dogwoods, flowering shrubs, iris, and other bulbs. They embellished the grounds with European statues which are still scattered throughout the garden amidst the many plantings. It seems that during the 1930s a grand total of 40 full-time gardeners was needed to tend the site. Unfortunately, the garden, which had been open to the public year-round, eventually went through periods of sad neglect; but today it is enjoying a renaissance, and calls itself "Louisiana's best kept secret garden." In addition to the scenic walk around the lake, you can enjoy miles of paths through woodlands of towering pines, cypress, poplars, oaks, and magnolias.

Many

Hodges Gardens
Highway 171 south of Many
Many, LA 71449

Tel. (318) 586-3523
Open: daily, dawn to dusk,
    except Christmas and
    New Year's
Fee

Hodges Gardens, situated within an abandoned stone quarry in the low, rolling pine hills of western Louisiana, was the creation of A.J. and Nona Trigg Hodges, two forward-thinking conservationists. In the 1940s, when few others were concerned about the consequences of deforestation, they purchased a 4,700-acre tract of land on a ridge to create an experimental arboretum. Within it was a stone quarry rich with wild flowers, unusually shaped rocks, and seedling pines, which was found to be an ideal spot for a woodland garden. They created a 225-acre lake, streams, walks, and foot bridges, and an animal haven with mostly elk and deer.

The garden (referred to as "a garden in the forest") includes some 70 acres, carefully landscaped to accentuate the dramatic rock formations and different levels of the terrain. The many flowerbeds (almost 100) are in bloom for most of the year. In spring you can enjoy a lovely rose garden on a slope above the lake, as well as plantings of tulips, bulbs, pansies, anemones, and flowering trees and shrubs. In summer, hydrangeas and water lilies reign; in autumn, chrysanthemums; and in winter, camellias. A conservatory and greenhouses contain palms, orchids, and bromeliads, among other exotic plants.

There are miles of drives past scenic points (don't miss the extraordinary view from Observation Point over the pine tops and lake, into East Texas) and hiking trails through the woods. An unexpected and interesting feature is an unusual remnant from the past: a 40-foot petrified tree trunk, thought to be an ancestor of the avocado, and probably thousands of years old.

New Iberia

Live Oaks Gardens
  (Rip Van Winkle Gardens)
5505 Rip Van Winkle Road
New Iberia, LA 70560

Tel. (337) 365-3332
Open: daily 9–5
Fee

Set deep into Cajun country, on a 25-acre salt dome surrounded by the flat marshlands typical of the region, these romantic English gardens are on a site claiming an intriguing past. Here, a pirate named Jean Lafitte once sought refuge and, according to local lore, buried his treasure. Then, in the nineteenth century the "island" became the winter retreat of Joseph Jefferson, the highly regarded American actor, famous for portraying Rip Van Winkle. He built a charming house, now the garden's museum, in a style reflecting Moorish architectural details he had noted while visiting his friend Washington Irving in Spain. And, apparently, President Grover Cleveland used to visit here, taking his naps in the cool shade of the live oak trees near the house. But it was not until the Bayless family bought the property in 1917 that the gardens actually came into being.

Live Oaks Gardens are so called because of the magnificent, gnarled and weathered specimens found here, some dating back 300 years. (Two are named for the pirate Lafitte, whose mysterious pots of old coins were supposedly once found nearby.) The gardens surround the house and, combining English naturalism with a lush, moss-draped exotic ambiance, are a delight to explore.

Paths (some through thick, tropical growth) lead to a secluded iris garden surrounded by bamboo; an "Alhambra" garden with terraces and pools; a camellia garden; an allée prettily framed with spring and summer blossoms; a magnolia walk; a rock garden; and a small Japanese tea garden, with lovely water views over a lagoon and lake. Traditional plants—roses, camellias, and azaleas—blend in gracefully with oleanders, gardenias, and hibiscus, and there are broad lawns with vistas, and a tropical glen. You will find something to enjoy year-round, whether in the inviting outdoor gardens or in the greenhouses whose collections of orchids, camellias, and tropical plants are well worth a visit.

Shadows-on-the-Teche　　　　*Tel. (337) 369-6446*
317 East Main Street　　　　*Open: daily 9–4:30*
New Iberia, LA 70560　　　　*Fee*

"The Shadows," now a historic National Trust site, includes a gracious 1830s plantation house surrounded by a lush, secluded garden. The two-and-a-half-acre property, once part of a much larger (158-acre) sugar cane plantation, is enclosed within rich clusters of bamboo and thick, green foliage. Within are inviting shaded pathways beneath massive live oaks draped with Spanish moss.

The present garden was created in the 1920s by William Weeks Hall, great-grandson of the original family owners. A keen enthusiast of landscape design (he was, in fact, a painter), he restored the badly overgrown landscape, transforming it from a basically functional property with just a few decorative gardens to an exclusively aesthetic pleasure.

In front of the house, considered one of the best examples of plantation house architecture in the country, are the magnificent live oaks, as well as collections of camellias and aspidistra. A small formal garden on the side of the house features elephant ears and yet more camellias, with a backdrop of Southern magnolias. The garden behind the house is built around a Victorian-style summer house along the bayou. Among the plant groupings are shell ginger, sweet olives, crape myrtles, rice paper plants, and azaleas. A well documented and informative guided tour conducts you through the house and gardens, but you can also walk around the grounds on your own.

New Orleans

Longue Vue Gardens
7 Bamboo Road
New Orleans, LA 70124

Tel. (504) 488-5488
Open: Mon.–Sat. 10–4:30;
  Sun. 1–5, except holidays
Fee

Here, on the outskirts of this romantic, historic city is a garden of water delights. Designed with Moorish features reminiscent of the Alhambra and Generalife Gardens in Granada, Longue Vue includes, among its pleasures, a formal court with reflecting pool and jets, canals, and many, many fountains—23, in fact!

In the early 1940s Edith and Edgar Stern decided to complement their Greek Revival mansion with an elegant formal garden. The deliciously cooling waterworks that make the garden so special and inviting, especially during the sultry Louisiana summers, were actually added later, in the mid-1960s.

The gardens are mostly divided into "rooms." A welcoming allée of oaks leads to the grand house and terrace overlooking the gardens. The central focus of the grounds is the Spanish Court. Surrounded by the shade of a loggia, it is graced with a rectangular mirror-like pool, in which delicate fountains make a gracefully arched pattern. On both sides of the Court are enclosed boxwood gardens with colorful potted plants and fountains, some replicas of those in the Alhambra.

Longue Vue also includes gardens that are not in the Spanish mode, such as a wildflower garden (with native varieties), a yellow flower garden, and a "Pan" garden. The brand new Discovery Garden is dedicated to children who want to learn about gardens in a hands-on fashion: here they can dig and discover natural pleasures on their own.

New Orleans Botanical Garden
City Park, 1 Palm Drive
New Orleans, LA 70124

Tel. (504) 483-9386
Open: Tues.–Sun. 10–4:30
Fee

This lovely botanical garden, the only one of its kind in Louisiana, features a vast collection of trees, shrubs, and flowers that thrive in this semitropical environment. Set within a public park that was once the site of a large plantation, it was created as a WPA project during the Depression. It contains some 2,000 varieties.

Majestic live oaks—the kind you picture when thinking of Southern landscapes—are among the garden's many offerings. These include secluded "rooms" enclosed with white camellia sasanqua, a water lily pond, fountains, statuary, and a formal parterre of roses in geometric patterns. There is a butterfly walk, too, as well as an aromatic garden featuring ginger and herbs. A lovely azalea garden complemented by magnolias and camellias has recently been added on the eastern end of the garden. A well-equipped Conservatory contains orchids, ferns, bromeliads, and other tropical examples that can be enjoyed year-round.

Old Ursuline Convent
1100 Chartres Street
New Orleans, LA 70116

Tel. (504) 529-3040
Open: guided tours hourly,
Tues.–Fri. 10–3; Sat. and
Sun. 11:15, 1, and 2
Fee

The Old Ursuline Convent, the oldest remaining building in the Mississippi Valley and now a Federal landmark, is among the city's most important historic relics. Located within the French Quarter, it is also among its most picturesque.

Its long and fascinating history reflects the turbulent events—fires, hurricanes, battles, massacres—that engaged New Orleans from its very beginnings. Here the dedicated and indefatigable nuns took in orphaned children, tended the sick and poor, and taught and counseled the young. When the nuns were moved to a new convent in 1824, the site became the home of the Bishop. It was not until 1941 that the existing garden was laid out.

The garden was based on plans from the old Royal Botanical Gardens that once existed across the street. Comprising six geometrically shaped parterres with carefully clipped borders in the formal eighteenth-century style, it was the work of the local garden club. The city agreed to maintain it, provided that the garden be open to the public.

A guided tour will take you through the garden, the Old Ursuline Convent, and the adjacent St. Mary's Church, also of historic significance.

St. Francisville

Afton Villa
U.S. Highway 61
St. Francisville, LA 70775

Tel. (504) 635-6773
Open: March–June and
Oct.–Nov., daily 9–4:30
Fee

Afton Villa is that quintessentially romantic Southern garden, complete with a welcoming allée of live oaks laced with Spanish moss, lush plantings amid languid statues, and the haunting atmosphere of an evocative past, which even includes a forlorn family cemetery. On this spot, over a century ago, a 40-room Gothic Revival mansion was built with extensive formal gardens that terraced down into a ravine. Over the years the house and garden underwent cycles of neglect and restoration until, in the 1970s, the garden at least was brought back to life.

Using the unearthed brick and stucco remains of the mansion as its framework, the new owners created a 10-acre formal garden surrounded by natural parkland. (The actual ruins of the old plantation house now contain a courtyard garden.) The formal area includes five terraces enclosed with traditional boxwood hedges, connected with stone steps and brick walkways. The first of these "rooms" is a colorful parterre of tulips, daylilies, and camellias, while others combine Italian marble statues with the plantings.

Beyond the sweetly fragrant gardens and green lawns lie the woodlands. Here, live oaks, wisteria, tulip trees, and cedars are interspersed with literally thousands of azaleas. An interesting historic footnote holds that these colorful azaleas are the actual descendants of a lone survivor of past gardens, known as "The pride of Afton."

Rosedown Plantation
and Gardens
12501 State Highway 10
St. Francisville, LA 70775

Tel.(504) 635-3332
Open: March–Oct., daily 9–5;
Nov.–Feb., daily, 10–4
Fee

Rosedown Plantation and Gardens, a 28-acre antebellum site, reflects Old South culture both in its elegant mansion and surrounding grounds. The elaborate gardens, a combination of seventeenth-century-style French gardens and more naturalistic English gardens, still contain some of the original plantings, making them among the nation's most important historic plant collections. Representing well over 150 years of continuous operation, they are also among the nation's oldest gardens.

Situated along a picturesque road once dotted with other prosperous plantations, the gardens were the creation of Martha and Daniel Turnbull. Like other Southern gentry, they had traveled throughout Europe partly in search of beautiful art objects and antiquities. (Many of the statues they collected on these trips are still found on the grounds.) Martha's horticultural abilities were considerable for her time, as she meticulously planned, then maintained for many years—eventually, all by herself—her gardens. Fortunately, she also kept a detailed garden journal, one that proved to be very useful in recreating the gardens after their inevitable decline many years later, in the 1950s.

Among Rosedown's special offerings are its magnificent rose gardens. These contain antique specimens, rarely found in modern rose gardens, including burr roses (called "chinquapin" roses in the South) and China roses. Also not to be missed are the camellia, azalea, and cryptomeria collections (the Turnbulls were among the earliest to import these specialties, and some of the azalea plants are over 100 years old); the fern gardens; and the herb and medicinal gardens. And, not surprisingly, here, too, is that gracious icon of many Southern plantations: a magnificent avenue of live oaks, some 200 years old, welcoming visitors to the house and gardens.

Shreveport

The Gardens of The American
Rose Center
8877 Jefferson-Paige Road
Shreveport, LA 71119

Tel. (318) 938-5402
Open: April–Oct., Mon.–Fri. 9–5;
Sat. and Sun. 9 to dusk
Fee

If you are a particular fan of roses, you won't want to miss these gardens. Comprising 42 acres surrounded by woodlands, they are, after all, the showcase for the American Rose Society. As such, they offer 20,000 (at last count) rose bushes divided into 60 individual gardens representing 450 varieties.

The site, a tribute to America's favorite flower, includes every name in the rosarian lexicon you could possibly come up with, from the All-America Rose Selections to miniature roses and the latest in hybrids. But this is more than just an outdoor museum: amateur gardeners wanting practical ideas for their own backyards can visit its more intimate theme gardens, oriented to family needs.

MISSISSIPPI

Belzoni
Biloxi
Greenwood
Jackson
Lucedale
Natchez
Oxford
Picayune
Woodville

1. Belzoni: Wister Gardens
2. Biloxi: Beauvoir
3. Greenwood: Florewood River Plantation State Park
4. Jackson: Mynelle Gardens
5. Lucedale: Palestinian Gardens
6. Natchez: Monmouth Plantation
7. Natchez: Stanton Hall Gardens
8. Oxford: Rowan Oak
9. Picayune: The Crosby Arboretum
10. Woodville: Rosemont Plantation

Belzoni

Wister Gardens
500 Henry Road
Belzoni, MS 39038

Tel. (662) 247-3025
Open: daily 8–5
Free

This is an elegantly landscaped, lush 14-acre estate surrounding a colonial house. There are broad lawns and a small decorative lake (populated by black swans, African geese, and flamingos). Wister Gardens has a nice deep-South ambiance with gazebos and serpentine paths through the trees. Some 8,000 azaleas bloom here in springtime, as do numerous bulbs (including 4,000 tulips), and a variety of lovely fruit trees. There are more than 120 varieties of trees and shrubs here. Also of note are the chrysanthemums of autumn and the camellia displays in winter.

Biloxi

Beauvoir
2244 Beach Boulevard (U.S. 90)
Biloxi, MS 39531

Tel. (228) 388-1313
Open: daily 8:30–5, except
     Christmas
Fee

Beauvoir is, of course, more than a garden. The Jefferson Davis Shrine and home here remind us that this is where the Confederate president spent the last 12 years of his life. For half a century afterward Beauvoir served as a home for Confederate veterans and widows. There are also two museums and a Confederate graveyard. This will be a visit in which the historic ambiance is very powerful.

The 57 acres of gardens seem appropriately old and lovely to look at. Until 1969 and a devastating hurricane, these were the same gardens that Jefferson Davis enjoyed walking through (and gardening in). But the original garden was under four feet of water after the storm and has taken decades of reworking, including the replacing of soil.

Today, once again, azaleas, roses, and camellias bloom in a naturalized setting. The garden court is semi-formal, with brick walks and brick-edged flowerbeds; there are no hedges or boxwood to break the openness of the setting. You'll find a judiciously placed bird-of-paradise in a decorative pot here and there, hibiscus and ferns, and palm and bamboo lending a tropical air. The peak time for a visit is spring. Plan on a nice walk!

Greenwood

Florewood River Plantation
  State Park
U.S. Highway 82
Greenwood, MS 38930

Tel. (662) 455-3821
Open: Tues.–Sat. 9–5 and Sun.
  1–5, except major holidays
Fee

This reconstruction of an 1850s Mississippi plantation is situated on 100 acres near the Yazoo River, in the heart of "cotton country." Here you'll find a fully revived picture of the nineteenth-century Delta cotton industry, from the reconstructed mansion to the museum with the Whitney gin, the smokehouse, blacksmith's, potter's and candlemaker's shops, and demonstrations in ante-bellum costumes. (In addition to touring the plantation, you can help pick cotton balls in the fall.)

Of particular interest to us, of course, are the gardens, set in the parklike grounds surrounding the mansion. They are pleasingly planted with Japanese boxwood, crape myrtle, live oak, peach, pear, dwarf plum trees, and southern wax myrtle. There are also vegetable gardens, and vast fields of cotton, corn, sorghum, and peas.

Jackson

Mynelle Gardens
4736 Clinton Boulevard
Jackson, MS 39209

Tel. (601) 960-1894
Open: March–Oct., 9–5;
  Nov.–Feb., 8–4:15
Fee

This is a seven-acre informal garden, with a delightful air all its own. Developed in 1920, by a noted local gardener named Mrs. Mynelle Westbrook Haywood (and since 1973 owned by the city of Jackson), Mynelle Gardens has a collection of Mississippi favorites planted in a series of lush and picturesque settings. Among them are an English Bog Garden, a Medical and Herb Garden, a Rustic Garden, an Old-fashioned Garden, and its pièce de résistance: a Japanese Garden. Plantings range from amaryllis, daylilies, gardenias, dianthus, and camellias, to roses and Asiatic magnolias, to a number of rare and ancient specimens—some dating back to the seventeenth century. (This is the kind of pretty setting that suggests weddings!) There are several nice walks, as well as trails for the handicapped.

Lucedale

Palestinian Gardens
Route 9 (Box 792)
Lucedale, MS 39452

Tel. (601) 947-8422
Open: March–Nov., daily 8–4
Fee

This is one of those great oddities we come across as we travel the country: a 20-acre garden that is a scale model of the Holy Land. Here you'll find the plants mentioned in the Bible, as well as miniature replicas of such ancient cities as Jerusalem, Bethlehem, Capernaum, and Jericho. This nondenominational site is open to all, and is one of those gardens in which an abstract idea has been fully realized.

Natchez

Monmouth Plantation
36 Melrose Avenue
Natchez, MS 39120

Tel. (601) 442-5852
Open: daily 9:30–4:15,
*   except Christmas*
Fee

Monmouth, a fine house built in about 1818, was the home of a prominent Natchez citizen and Mexican War hero named General John Anthony Quitman and his wife, Eliza Turner Quitman. The general was known to be the richest man in Natchez in his day, and his antebellum house and gardens were suitably magnificent. Great oaks dripping with Spanish moss surrounded the house. He imported 40 trees and vines from France, grew peaches, pears, nectarines, olives, figs, and many flowers in separate formal beds. Even one of his gardeners was imported—from England.

Now a National Historic Landmark, Monmouth has had a long and colorful history, including terrible destruction during the Civil War, the burning of some of the great oaks for firewood, and a fall into decay and ruin. In 1977 the place was bought and restored by a couple from California, and today the reconstructed, replanted Monmouth is open to the public. Now, thoroughly and lovingly restored, Monmouth's gardens are a delight. Neat brick walks crisscross the grounds, while a gazebo and small pond add interest to the collection of flowers, especially the camellias.

(Natchez is noted for its antebellum houses and gardens. This garden, like Stanton Hall, below, and nearby Longwood can be visited all year. Other Natchez mansions and gardens—including Hope Farms, Rosalie, D'Evereux, and Cherokee—are open on special days in spring and fall; call Natchez Pilgrimage at 800-442-2011 for information on all of the city's historic houses and gardens.)

Stanton Hall Gardens	*Tel. (800) 647-6742*
401 High Street	*Open: daily 9–5*
Natchez, MS 39120	*Fee*

Dating from 1851, this is a fine antebellum mansion with grounds that feature live oak, azaleas, camellias, daylilies, caladiums, and other pleasures. The opulent, very elaborate, Greek Revival house is well worth a visit, with its great columns, imported marble mantels, chandeliers, and glamorous staircase. And it is appropriately located in an inviting deep-South garden setting. Visit in spring or summer for best viewing of flowering shrubbery under the live oaks.

Oxford

Rowan Oak	*Tel. (248) 234-3284*
Old Taylor Road	*Open: Tues.–Sat.10–noon*
Oxford, MS 38655	*and 2–4; Sun. 2–4*
	(closed university holidays)
	Free

If you are visiting Mississippi you will not want to miss William Faulkner's 1840s home and its garden at the University of Mississippi. It is now a National Historic Landmark. No recent figure is so identified with the state and its landscape as Faulkner, and here you will see not only the great writer's fine antebellum house with its columned portico and library and writing room (with his Underwood typewriter still in place), but also the lovely garden he created. The hedge-bordered rose garden is the high point of the tree-shaded outdoor setting, which also includes a stable and smokehouse.

Picayune

The Crosby Arboretum
370 Ridge Road
Picayune, MS 39466

Tel. (601) 799-2311
Open: Wed.–Sun. 9–5
Fee

The Crosby Arboretum is a fairly new garden center, with the admirable aim of specializing in plants native to its Pearl River habitat. Among its plantings are many delightful wildflowers, and in May it sponsors a wildflower weekend when thousands of them are in bloom. There are also many shrubs and trees planted here (most quite recently). Although it is just about 20 years old, the Arboretum already has extensive plantings and is planning on expansion.

Woodville

Rosemont Plantation
Highway 24 E (Main Street)
Woodville, MS 39669

Tel. (601) 888-6809
Open: March–Dec.15, Mon.–Fri.
Fee

The boyhood home of Jefferson Davis, Rosemont is a c.1810 modest "planter's cottage" set amid 300 acres of plantation lands and a charming garden. Five generations of the Davis family lived at Rosemont. The cool gardens are shaded by evergreen magnolias and great live oaks draped with Spanish moss. In spring and summer you'll see the tiny magenta roses that climb up the white latticework of the house; these are just part of the elaborate rose gardens originally planted in the early 1800s by Jane Davis, the Confederate president's mother.

NORTH CAROLINA

Asheville   Belmont

Boone   Chapel Hill

Charlotte   Clemmons

Clyde   Durham

Fayetteville   Greensboro

Manteo   New Bern

Pinehurst   Raleigh

Salisbury   Wilkesboro

Wilmington   Winnabow

Winston-Salem

1. Asheville: Biltmore Estate
2. Asheville: The Botanical Gardens at Asheville
3. Belmont: Daniel Stowe Botanical Garden
4. Boone: Daniel Boone Native Gardens
5. Chapel Hill: North Carolina Botanical Garden and Coker Arboretum
6. Charlotte: U.N.C. Charlotte Botanical Gardens
7. Charlotte: Wing Haven Gardens and Bird Sanctuary
8. Clemmons: Tanglewood Arboretum and Rose Garden
9. Clyde: Campus Arboretum of Haywood Community College
10. Durham: Sarah P. Duke Gardens
11. Fayetteville: Cape Fear Botanical Garden
12. Greensboro: Greensboro Arboretum
13. Greensboro: Greensboro Bicentennial Garden and Bog Garden
14. Manteo: Elizabethan Gardens
15. New Bern: Tryon Palace Gardens
16. Pinehurst: Sandhills Horticultural Gardens
17. Raleigh: J.C. Raulston Arboretum at N.C.S.U.
18. Raleigh: Raleigh Municipal Rose Garden
19. Salisbury: Elizabeth Holmes Hurley Park
20. Wilkesboro: Wilkes Community College Gardens
21. Wilmington: Airlie Gardens
22. Wilmington: Greenfield Gardens
23. Wilmington: New Hanover County Extension Service Arboretum
24. Winnabow: Orton Plantation Gardens
25. Winston-Salem: Old Salem Gardens
26. Winston-Salem: Reynolda Gardens at Wake Forest University

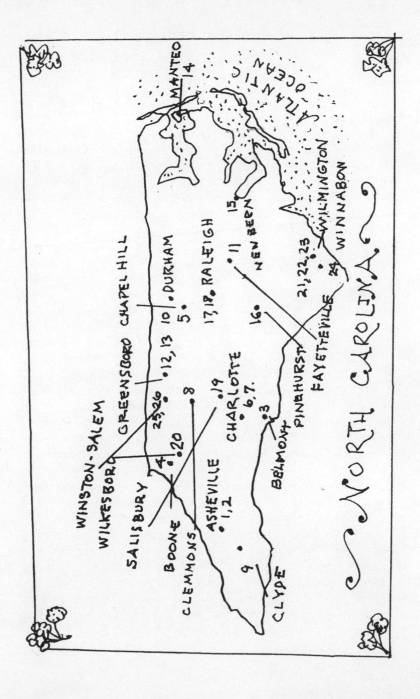

Asheville

Biltmore Estate
One North Pack Square
Asheville, NC 28801

Tel. (800) 543-2961
Open: daily 9–5; call for special
 hours and events
Fee

Biltmore Estate is not just a garden, though the gardens are well worth a visit on their own. The 250-room mansion remains the largest private residence in the United States, built for the grandson of Cornelius Vanderbilt. It is now a historic landmark, a turn-of-the-century Renaissance-style château in the heart of the Blue Ridge Mountains. You should certainly visit it when you come to see the gardens, since the fee covers Biltmore House, Gardens, and Winery.

The grounds, designed by America's master landscape architect, Frederick Law Olmsted, cover 8,000 acres of beautiful rolling terrain. With this kind of pedigree, Biltmore is clearly a garden lover's paradise. Huge, glamorous, partly formal and partly woodsy, the estate gardens truly have something for every taste. A few highpoints include the 50,000 spring bulbs in a walled garden (considered one of the finest English-style gardens in the nation) with tulips and daffodils planted in geometric color patterns. The same area is planted with summer annuals and myriad chrysanthemums in fall. There is a notable rose garden which displays 250 species, blooming from mid-spring through late fall. In the wooded areas there are azaleas, forsythia, and dogwoods aplenty, adorning the lovely landscape in the Azalea Garden and along the walkways. A formal Italian garden has three pools with aquatic plants (including Egyptian lotus and water lilies), statuary and benches.

A brief sketch of your visit might include beginning at the side of Biltmore House in the arbored terrace draped with three seasons of flowering vines and overlooking the formal Italian garden. A lush shrub garden, featuring huge banks of snowball viburnum and azaleas, borders the path to the great walled tulip garden and the magnificent rose garden. You will find the conservatory farther down the path, shielded from view by a tall holly hedge. Inside you'll find the Palm House, hydrangeas, orchids, and other delights. Next is the azalea garden (we visited in spring!) starring the Piedmont Azalea, native to the Blue Ridge area. A small creek with stepping stones and Japanese bridge leads to the woodsy landscape beyond.

All of the gardens are very accessible and inviting to wanderers. We judge a visit here to be a full day's adventure.

Botanical Gardens at Asheville   *Tel. (828) 252-5190*
(University of North Carolina)   *Open: daily 9:30–4:30*
151 W.T. Weaver Boulevard   *Free*
Asheville, NC 28804

Here, in this Southern Appalachian region, plants native to the area are preserved and showcased over 10 beautiful acres. A prize-winning garden for the blind and spectacular wildflower trails are among the many fine elements of these botanical gardens. Designed by noted landscape architect Doan Ogden (who also created the gardens at Haywood Community College in Clyde and the Daniel Boone Gardens in Boone), the overall ambiance is one of informality, with blooming rhododendrons, dogwoods, and other spring blooms in profusion. Specialties include a Sunshine Garden, an Azalea Garden, and a Sycamore Area. (You can also see earthworks from the Battle of Asheville.) There are many trails through meadows and woods. For best viewing visit between early April and mid-June, but at any time you'll find interesting things going on. There is a botany center and year-round activities, such as a three-day Annual Wildflower Pilgrimage.

Belmont

Daniel Stowe Botanical Garden   *Tel. (704) 825-4490*
6500 South New Hope Road   *Open: Mon.–Sat. 9–5; Sun. 12–5;*
Belmont, NC 28012-9906   *closed Christmas Day*
                                                 Free

This is a very new garden, but the aim of its creator (a retired executive named Daniel Stowe) to create a vibrant Conservancy and large public garden, is already evident. Eventually some 400 acres will be included. Phase One—the ten acres already landscaped and cultivated—offers fine display gardens, conservatories, many water features, and lots of birds. Specialties include daylilies, native plants and shrubs, a kitchen garden, and all kinds of seasonal plantings. You'll find a children's garden, a gazebo, a knot garden, several border gardens arranged by color, and a butterfly garden, among other completed areas.

It is always interesting to see a great garden in its early stages, and this one is already well on its way, though still in a somewhat unfinished state (with a fair amount of work going on while we were there). Best time to visit is springtime.

Boone

Daniel Boone Native Gardens
Route 421/321(west of Blue
   Ridge Parkway)
Boone, NC 28607

Tel. (828) 264-6390
Open: May through Oct., daily
   9–6, weather permitting
Fee

These 10 acres are a good place for a self-guided tour. A brochure is available at the entrance, and you can wander through the native North Carolina plantings, identifying plants as you go. The designer was Doan Ogden (the creator of distinctive gardens at Asheville and Clyde, North Carolina.) Named for Daniel Boone, the frontiersman and explorer (whose hand-hewn log cabin is here), the gardens are informal and very pretty, with pools, meadows, a sunken garden, a bog garden, a fern garden, a rock garden and a meditation garden. Specialties include native flora like azaleas, honeysuckle, clematis, dogwood, Black Mountain heart cherry, wildflowers, and a variety of other blooms that make this section of the state so delectable in springtime.

Chapel Hill

North Carolina Botanical
   Garden and Coker Arboretum
University of North Carolina
Laurel Hill Road
Chapel Hill, NC 27599

Tel. (919) 962-0522
Open: daily, dawn to dusk
Free

The University of North Carolina's Botanical Garden is actually made up of two separate sites: the Coker Arboretum—in the center of the campus—and a large woodland and demonstration and research garden complex. Each site is enjoyable in its own way. Together they add up to some 600 acres of plantings.

The Coker Arboretum, which is next to the Planetarium in the heart of the campus, is a very informal setting rather like a good-sized city park. Once a pasture, the space was converted by a professor of botany, William Coker, beginning almost a century ago. Professor Coker wanted an area to preserve North Carolina's native shrubs, trees, and flowers, and that is just what this arboretum does, in a charming, rather overgrown way. Don't miss the great wisteria arbor that runs the entire length of one side (visit in spring), the camellia collection, sweet-breath-of-spring, and a variety of other blooms. Amid the nice sandy paths and moss-covered walls, are wonderful, very tall trees, including some unusual ones: the dove tree, Chinese fringetree, Chinese pistachio, Japanese plum yew, as well as the lovely crape myrtle, bald cypress, and Marshall's hawthorn. Pick up a guide to the many trees, each of which is numbered. There are also many, many birds.

The Botanical Garden on Laurel Hill Road is a research and teaching facility, with a large area of different types of plantings and collections, many of them nicely obscure or unusual; a carnivorous garden, an aquatic collection, a knot garden, and a series of different habitat gardens, among others. You can enjoy these different sites in a variety of ways, and if you are a gardener yourself, they are particularly interesting because the emphasis is on learning the ins and outs of gardening (there are numerous events and classes here), from fertilizer to container gardening. But parts of it are also very lovely to look at too.

Charlotte

U.N.C. Charlotte Botanical
   Gardens
Mary Alexander Road and
   Craven Road
Charlotte, NC 28223

Tel. (704) 547-4055
Open: gardens daily, sunrise
   to sunset; greenhouses
   Mon.–Fri. 9–4, Sat. 10–3
Free

This is a nine-acre garden a little more than 30 years old, with greenhouses and several specialty gardens. The greenhouses, which have 4,000 square feet of space, feature five distinct growing environments, including a rain forest and herbarium, and collections of succulents, orchids, and pitcher plants among the most popular. The herbarium contains over 20,000 preserved specimens of native and non-native plants.

The outdoor specialty gardens are devoted to North Carolina native plants, rhododendron hybrids, and hardy ornamentals, and some 50 species of ferns. Of particular charm is the Van Landingham Glen, named for the rhododendron enthusiast who planted it; this is one of the largest collections of rhododendrons in the Southeast, numbering in the thousands. Also of note is the Susie Harwood Garden with its lushly overgrown steps and moon gate. This rather Asian-in-style, three-acre garden has an aquatic section, an area of perennials, and all-season plantings.

Pick up a self-guiding brochure at the greenhouses before you set out on the very beautiful outing through the gardens.

Wing Haven Gardens and   *Tel. (704) 331-0664*
* Bird Sanctuary*   *Open: Tues. and Wed. 3–5;*
248 Ridgewood Avenue   *Sun. 2–5*
Charlotte, NC 28209-1632   *Free*

Situated in an old Charlotte neighborhood, Wing Haven is a three-acre walled delight, densely planted by the owners, Elizabeth and Edwin Clarkson, starting back in 1927. A tiny wilderness and sanctuary (birds have always loved the spot, and indeed an orphaned bluebird had the run of the house and bathed in the bathroom!), Wing Haven is one of those special gardens with its own ambiance. There are birdbaths and fountains among the flowers, a formal garden, a rose garden, woodland shrubs, and a variety of lovely ornamental, and pleasantly uneven brick paths and plazas with benches, a sundial, and oval reflecting pool.

This is an old garden, and it has the great trees (though Hurricane Hugo brought down 75 of them, many now replaced), the aged brick, and the statuary and plantings of a traditional Southern garden. There are tunnels of ivy, wooden arbors, wildflowers, an herb garden with 75 different kinds of herbs, boxwood hedges, a camellia collection, ducks that wander through the garden, and wonderful birdcalls throughout. In fact, all of the plantings had the pleasure of birds in mind, from water elements to nesting spots to favorite foods.

A visit here makes you feel like a privileged visitor to a private garden. The brochure for the Wing Haven Foundation (which now runs the gardens) quotes the great garden designer Gertrude Jekyll: "I hold the firm belief that the purpose of a garden is to give happiness and repose of mind." Wing Haven is a perfect case in point.

Clemmons

Tanglewood Arboretum and
  Rose Garden
U.S. Highway 158
Clemmons, NC 27012

Tel. (336) 766-0591
Open: daily 8 A.M. to dusk
Fee to park

Located in a large recreational complex called Tanglewood Park, these gardens are just one section of the large entertainment area (race track, golf course, campground, etc.). But here you'll find a most unusual arboretum that specializes in Piedmont trees, and a fine rose garden. The land was left to the public by one of the Reynolds (tobacco) family, and the handiwork of Frank Lustig, a Reynolds family gardener, can be seen in the fine landscaping.

The arboretum, which features oak and black walnut, flowering native trees (dogwoods, azaleas, rhododendrons, burning bush, etc.), also contains specimens from around the world. The rose garden has some 800 plants. There is also a hedged fragrance garden, and a self-guided nature trail with audio stations for the blind.

Clyde

Campus Arboretum of Haywood
  Community College
Freedlander Drive,
  (west of Asheville)
Clyde, NC 28721

Tel. (828) 672-2821
Open: Mon.–Fri. 8–11; Sat 8–4;
  closed Sundays
Free

This fairly new, 80-acre campus has made a point of turning much of its open space into garden areas. The school hired the noted landscape architect, Doan Ogden, to create a master landscape plan for the campus, set in what was once a farm, beautifully located in the Southern Appalachians. (Other gardens designed by Ogden are in Boone, and Belmont, North Carolina.)

Ogden's accomplishment includes a fine series of flower gardens (including a dahlia garden, an Oriental Garden, and a rose garden), a preserved native forest, a wonderful variety of trees (including a willow walk), and one of the best rhododendron collections in this western region of North Carolina. Don't miss the "tunnel walk" through the laburnum trees, or the outdoor circular classroom surrounded by boxwoods. There are many more garden delights here (kept up by horticulture students). Western North Carolina is a very pretty part of the world, particularly in springtime, and this campus has truly captured the natural beauty of its surroundings.

Durham

Sarah P. Duke Gardens
Duke University
Durham, NC 27708

Tel. (919) 684-3698
Open: daily 8 A.M. to sunset
Free

One of the best known of Southern gardens, the Sarah P. Duke Gardens can best be described as grand. Though originally planned for the use of the Duke University community, the impressive gardens were opened to the public, which takes full advantage of them: some 200,000 visitors come each year. But these 55 acres are large enough to accommodate everyone without crowding, and you'll find lots to catch your eye as you walk through the five miles (!) of carefully marked pathways from one scenic beauty to the next. The gardens are divided into both wooded and formal areas: twenty acres are developed, and thirty-five are native woodland, mostly pine forests. There are more than 2,000 species of plants in these acres.

We found the most spectacular part of the gardens to be the great hillside Terrace Garden, which was commissioned by Mary Duke Biddle in honor of her mother Sarah P. Duke, who financed the original gardens. The design was by Ellen Biddle Shipman; her terraced layout has become something of a landmark among eastern and southern gardens. The Terraces, as they are known, are giant—an entire hillside of blooms divided by terracing rock walls. Between the flagstone walls are rows and rows of bulbs and seasonal flowers. (From the bottom looking up, you feel as though you are in an amphitheater of blooms, with each flower neatly in place, like an audience!) This is truly a sight to see. Among the glories of The Terraces are an octagonal Chinese wisteria pergola at the top, and the flowering trees interspersed among the flowers: ornamental cherry, dogwood, redbud, and crab apple. At the bottom of this garden is a naturalistic pool, with water lilies and goldfish. Stretching beyond it are open fields.

Major garden areas are devoted to irises, azaleas, peonies, holly, and in fall some 7,000 chrysanthemums. (You can visit this site year-round and always find something blooming.) There is a walled, circular rose garden, a garden of native plants (some 600 species), and a bog garden where you may spot a Venus flytrap.

Another extraordinary pleasure of the gardens is the Asiatic Arboretum, a newly developed and very beautiful 20-acre area, with water, bamboo, forsythia, rocks, and a general atmosphere of serenity. This large area is particularly quiet and pretty.

Our overall impression of these gardens was one of grandeur and magnificence from the moment you enter the imposing wrought-iron gates and are greeted by a vast formal bed of blooming flowers (hundreds and hundreds of bright tulips when we were there). Students and other members of the university community have a most extraordinary place to study outdoors!

Fayetteville

Cape Fear Botanical Garden　　*Tel. (910) 486-0221*
536 North Eastern Boulevard　*Open: Mon.–Sat. 10–5; Sun.*
Fayetteville, NC 28305　　　　*noon to 5; closed mid-Dec.*
　　　　　　　　　　　　　　　to mid-Feb.
　　　　　　　　　　　　　　　Fee

There are 85 acres in this botanical garden bordering the Cape Fear River. Ranging from formal plantings to trails through a wilderness, these acres will suit a variety of tastes. There are some terrific views (take the trails to bluffs that overlook the Cape Fear River and a nearby meandering stream called Cross Creek). You will also find a natural amphitheater here, and a series of well-kept flower gardens, as well. The combining of wilderness trails and formal gardens is increasingly popular in botanical gardens like these, giving lovers of both cultivated flowers and natural plantings plenty to enjoy.

Greensboro

Greensboro Arboretum　　*Tel. (336) 373-2558*
West Market Street　　　*Open: daily, sunrise to sunset*
Greensboro, NC 27402　　*Free*

Greensboro Beautiful, Inc. is an organization that works to beautify its city. There are three major sites: the Arboretum, the Bog Garden, and the Bicentennial Garden (see below). The Arboretum, though primarily a wooded, 17-acre site, also features a number of specialty gardens, including a Butterfly Garden with fountain, a Winter Garden, a Ground Cover Garden, a Hydrophytic Garden (aquatic plants), a vine garden, a Rhododendron Garden, and many trails through wildflowers—both native and exotic. This is a lovely place for a walk.

Greensboro Bicentennial Garden   *Tel. (336) 373-2558*
   and Bog Garden   *Open: daily, sunrise to sunset*
1105 Hobbs Road   *Free*
Greensboro, NC 27402

The Bicentennial Garden consists of seven and a half acres of year-round formal gardens, with bulb and annual beds, a rose garden, two rock gardens, and a variety of other pleasures, including a fragrance garden for the blind. The spring bulb garden has over 30,000 plants! There are 105 varieties of daylilies here. There are also a camellia and azalea collection, and an overall ambiance of brilliant color and pleasant design. Best viewing is in springtime and summer. You may well spot a wedding here among the flowers.

Just across the street is the Bog Garden, adjacent to a lake. Here you'll discover a wild bog and an elevated wooden walkway, which leads you through the marshy land to see its indigenous plants and wildlife. There are stands of bamboo, ferns, wildflowers, and a variety of wild ducks and fish.

The two gardens and arboretum of Greensboro Beautiful, Inc. can be visited on one outing, and are excellent examples of how a city and its residents can take undeveloped land and join together to maintain public gardens for the enjoyment of all.

Manteo

Elizabethan Gardens   *Tel. (252) 473-3234*
Highway 64/264   *Open: daily 9–5*
Manteo, Roanoke Island, NC *Fee*
   27954

In our myriad visits to so many gardens, a few stand out as very special places that capture some intangible quality of design and history, a delicate ambiance that makes them special. This is truly one of the most beautiful gardens of all. This 10-acre garden is an artist's dream. The layout centers around a great empty lawn, but everywhere there are curving, twisting shapes of tree limbs: crape myrtle and live oaks. Their branches make sweeping forms reminiscent of van Gogh, a stunning contrast with the formal straight lines of stone balustrades and parterre gardens of geometric beds outlined neatly in boxwood. Throughout the gardens are inviting vistas in every direction, from overlooks of beach and water (we are on an island) to arched lookouts, to a sunken garden, through a great tightly-knit holly allée. You will not often find a garden that is so imaginatively conceived as this one.

Elizabethan Gardens are on the site of the first English colony (1587) in the New World, the ill-fated Roanoke colony. The gardens, in a style reminiscent of sixteenth-century English pleasure gardens, were created in 1951 by two well-known landscape designers, Richard Webel and M. Umberto Innocenti. Gifts, from John Hay Whitney, of antique British garden statuary and fountains—some actually dating to the fifteenth century—added to the historic nature of the design.

The plans included elements familiar to Elizabethan gardeners: a sunken garden, a rose garden, a thatched gazebo with a conical roof, marble fountains and balustrades, a mix of culinary and decorative plantings, an herb garden (with Shakespearean quotations), a sundial, and a Gate House patterned after a sixteenth century orangery. A water gate marks the spot where the colonists are thought to have come ashore. Punctuating the entire acreage are great trees (there is an ancient oak from the sixteenth century) and massive shrubs (hibiscus, rhododendrons, camellias, etc.) that are stunningly lush in blooming season.

Among our favorite spots was the sunken garden surrounded by a holly allée, some 10 or 11 feet high, with long shady paths surrounding an open garden and a central fountain. Another was the amazing camellia collection, through which one could stroll on pine-needle paths. The crape myrtle trees with their bright pink blossoms and gnarled white branches are an integral part of these gardens, creating a glorious, decorative setting for plantings ranging from wildflowers (including wild orchids) to gardenias.

It is nice to imagine this lovely spot as a touch of home for the poor colonists who struggled to survive here, but in any case, it is a reminder of how far back the beauty of English garden design goes. Certainly the

Elizabethans knew a great deal about landscape and gardens—from both a practical and an aesthetic viewpoint. Don't miss this one!

New Bern

Tryon Palace Gardens
610 Pollock Street
New Bern, NC 28563

Tel. (252) 514-4900 or
(800) 767-1560
Open: Mon.–Sat. 9–4; Sun. 1–4;
closed some holidays
Fee

A thorough tour of Tryon Palace will take you through a grand historic site: the great building itself, a series of smaller structures, and all of their gardens. Georgian-style Tryon Palace sits proudly on the water's edge in the heart of New Bern. It has a long and illustrious history as the governor's seat of power before the Revolution and as a prime example of an "English" colonial estate. The palace's gardens, laid out in the 1770s, were elegant from the start. The palace and the gardens fell into disrepair, but their careful renovation gives us a revitalized mansion and 14 acres of landscaping to enjoy.

The gardens at the palace are actually a collection of different settings, many of them bordered by the brick wings and walls of the palace. Since no plan remained of the original gardens, they have been restored in a variety of styles, ranging from the simple colonial Kitchen Garden to formal elegance more reminiscent of the Victorian era. But most of the trees and flowers are known to have been used in the United States in the eighteenth century, and many British gardens of the period were studied for the restoration.

Highpoints include the fine brick walls, paths, antique statuary, white marble classical temple, wrought-iron gates, espaliered fruit trees, round topiary forms, and a pretty parterre garden with a series of arabesques of boxwood, filled with flowers (hundreds of tulips at our visit). These small garden settings are interspersed with a large open lawn (with water view), a wilderness area, two parallel allées, and continuous walkways (where you can occasionally see employees of the palace in colonial dress). The gardens are best beginning in April.

Pinehurst

Sandhills Horticultural Gardens
2200 Airport Road
Pinehurst, NC 28374-8299

Tel. (910) 695-3882
Open: daylight hours
Free

Demonstration gardens here are part of the horticultural program at Sandhills Community College. They are maintained by the students and faculty of the Landscape Gardening School and the community. Highpoints of the 25-acre landscape are the unusually extensive holly garden (some 350 different cultivars and a real maze—take the kids), and a boardwalk through the Wetlands Garden. Other specialty gardens include the wonderfully named Sir Walter Raleigh Garden, a rose garden, and a conifer garden. One of the nicest aspects of this garden is the use of trellises and other decorative elements like fountains and nicely placed benches, waterfalls, bridges, and pools.

Raleigh

J.C. Raulston Arboretum
at N.C.S.U.
4301 Beryl Road
Raleigh, NC 27606

Tel. (919) 515-3132
Open: daily 8 A.M. to sunset
Free

The State University has two separate—both interesting—garden areas to visit. This eight-acre arboretum, which is about 20 years old, is used by the horticultural program at the university, and serves as an outdoor classroom and demonstration garden. It was the pet project of Dr. J.C. Raulston, a professor of horticulture at the university, who wanted to expand the vistas of North Carolina gardeners.

In addition to its useful aspects as a research and teaching facility, this large, flat arboretum has a number of specialty gardens that are quite lovely to look at. Our favorite was the Shade House, a slatted-walled garden. This unusual space is quite large, with delicate, flickering sunlight that shines through the thin wooden slatted walls onto some 1,500 different plants that thrive in shady climates. There is a somewhat Asian atmosphere here, and it is well worth a visit.

Other specialty areas include gardens devoted to roses and magnolias, a Victorian Gazebo, a Zen Garden, a Paradise Garden, a White Garden, a Reading Garden, an Edible Garden, a fern collection, and a variety of North Carolina trees, including crape myrtle, junipers, dwarf loblolly pine, the world's largest collection of redbud trees. Some 6,000 different species from 55 countries are planted here, and just about all of them are labeled.

A perennial garden has thousands of blooms within a 450-foot long border; the pattern follows the precepts of the great landscape designer Gertrude Jekyll. (It was described by noted British Landscape architect Sir Geoffrey Jellicoe as "an epic border, a heroic event in landscape architecture.") It is at its best from May to November.

In keeping with its function as a teaching and research facility, there is little overall design tying these many gardens together. But each individual part is well thought out and attractive, and you'll enjoy the variety; it is almost like walking through a garden bazaar. If you are a gardener this is a very useful spot, since material about how to grow the plants you see is available at the entrance.

Raleigh Municipal Rose Garden   *Tel. (919) 831-6840*
Pogue Street   *Open: daily, daylight hours*
Raleigh, NC 27650   *Free*

This rose garden is set on a charming six-and-a-half-acre, hilly site behind a theater of the University—in fact, the garden shares the dell with an amphitheater. It is unpretentious in design, but its terraced feeling, and a variety of delicious plantings make it quite lovely. If you like rose gardens, you'll find this one unusually pleasing. Though it is open year-round, and has some additional types of plantings, rose enthusiasts should visit from mid-May until late fall.

Salisbury

Elizabeth Holmes Hurley Park   *Tel. (704) 638-5260*
Lake Drive   *Open: daily, sunrise to sunset*
Salisbury, NC 28145   *Free*

This is a 15-acre park that was carefully designed not very long ago—not as formal gardens, but as a year-round attraction with natural plantings for each season. The park features woodland trails, wildflowers, footbridges over water, and other quiet pleasures. Stroll here in spring for the lovely collection of flowering delights, such as azaleas and magnolias, perennial plantings, and the wildflowers dotted throughout the woods, and in winter for its outstanding red-berry holly collection. All the plants are labeled.

Wilkesboro

Wilkes Community College   *Tel. (336) 838-6294*
  Gardens   *Open: dawn to dusk*
Collegiate Road   *Free*
Wilkesboro, NC 28697

There are a number of specialty gardens on this 140-acre campus; among them are a Rose Garden, a Native Plant Garden, a Japanese Garden, a wildflower meadow, a Victory Vegetable Garden, and a distinctive Sensory Garden. Kept up with community support, including that of noted bluegrass musician "Doc" Watson, the gardens are the setting for an annual Bluegrass Festival. The Eddy Merle Watson Memorial Garden for the Senses includes a 70-foot concrete and brick wall with carvings to touch, the work of a local artist, Patricia Turlington. Children will enjoy a playground in the gardens.

Wilmington

Airlie Gardens   *Tel. (910) 763-4646*
Airlie Road off Rte. 76   *Open: March 1–Oct. 3, 8–6*
Wilmington, NC 28402   *Fee*

If your taste runs to the old and lush and naturalized in public gardens, visit Airlie Gardens. It is huge (155 acres—though about 50 of them are the primary garden area), gracious, pre-Civil War in design, and is sometimes described as a "paradise" on the North Carolina coast.

Its setting and history are both colorful. It sits along Bradley Creek and the Wrightsville Sound, overlooking Money Island, which is thought to be the site of Captain Kidd's buried treasure. In the nineteenth century the estate was owned by a wealthy rice plantation owner named Pembroke Jones, who named it after his ancestral home in Scotland. It was he who built the 35-room mansion and developed the gardens. Fortunately, its present owners, the Corbetts, have opened their elegant grounds to the public.

The pleasures of Airlie Gardens reflect the overall age and lushness of the landscape. There are azaleas and camellias in abundance (many reflected in the waters of a spring-fed garden lake), and great live oaks draped with Spanish moss. Swans glide under the flowering shrubs. There are many walking trails, a formal garden called the "Spring Garden," and an 1835 rural chapel, a pergola, and other delights. We suggest a visit in spring to see this place at its most breathtaking.

Greenfield Gardens   *Tel. (910) 341-7855*
302 Willard Street   *Open: dawn to dusk*
Wilmington, NC 28402   *Free*

Greenfield Gardens are part of Greenfield Park in the heart of this coastal city. Once a plantation, the park covers 180 acres. It offers a variety of recreational activities, including boating and a scenic drive around a lake, graced by the spectacular azalea collection, said to number in the thousands. (Call for the dates of their Azalea Festival each spring.) The formal plantings include many specialty areas, such as a fragrance garden, a summer annual garden, and a rose garden— maintained by civic associations. Throughout the park there are nature trails leading the visitor to spectacular examples of bald cypresses dripping with moss, crape myrtles (a personal favorite of ours), flowering trees including dogwoods—and those azaleas. Visit in early spring for this treat.

New Hanover County Extension   *Tel. (910) 452-6393*
*   Service Arboretum*   *Open: daily, sunrise to sunset*
6202 Oleander Drive   *Free*
Wilmington, NC 28403

Situated on the southeastern coast of North Carolina, this six-and-a-half-acre arboretum features plants that are best suited to the geographical conditions of coastal gardens. Among the 32 different gardens are several that will be of interest to local gardeners, as well as a conservatory with exotic plants from other regions, and even a miniature rain forest. Included in the specialty gardens are an aquatic garden, a perennial garden, a rose garden, and a shade garden. You can walk along paved pathways from garden to garden under the mature live oak trees.

Winnabow

Orton Plantation Gardens
9149 Orton Road, S.E.
Winnabow, NC 28479

Tel. (910) 371-6851
Open: March–Nov., daily 8–6
Fee

One of the only great plantation gardens open to the public in North Carolina, Orton's magnificent gardens were actually planted in this century around the family's historic antebellum home. This former rice plantation along the Cape Fear River (not far from Wilmington) covers 30 acres in a coastal area more typical of the Deep South than North Carolina. Although its once thriving rice production was abandoned in the late nineteenth century, the owners continued to flood the fields each winter. Migrating birds and other wildlife are abundant in this wildlife sanctuary.

In 1910 the first garden terraces were built by James and Luola Sprunt. They planted camellias, azaleas, rhododendrons, and banana shrubs. In the 1930s their son began the extensive landscaping of the estate, laying out the formal (and the natural) gardens that give the landscape its great beauty. Today, 20 of the acres form the well-known gardens. (The plantation house is still lived in by members of the original family and is not open to the public.)

A visit will take you into a world of lagoons and winding paths, belvederes and great live oaks draped with moss arching overhead, and a series of small, delightful gardens devoted to beautiful plantings—crape myrtles, hydrangeas, Cherokee roses, wisteria, camellias, oleander, magnolias, and other Southern specialties. Individual gardens are ornamental pleasures; among them are a Radial Garden, a Scroll Garden, a Sun Garden, and a Triangle Garden. Each of these design-oriented, well-kept sites has its own kinds of flowers and ambiance. Of particular note is the shade here, in this region of searing hot sunlight. The gardens are best from March through September. The first two weeks of April are the high point with a dazzling azalea display, but this garden also offers flowering trees and shrubs throughout the summer months.

The overall atmosphere is created by the juxtaposition of natural wetlands and lagoons and waterfowl and wildlife, with the elegance of formal gardens. (Not for the faint of heart, these gardens, with their low bridges and walkways, are just above water—and alligator—level.) Orton's gardens will make a vivid impression, evoking both the beauty of the Old South with its plantation culture, and the bright face and hidden dangers of the tropics. As you stroll among the great oaks, or over a Chinese bridge, or through the colonial cemetery, or as you watch for water birds from a belvedere over a lagoon, you will be transported to another time and place. A great garden can do that.

Winston-Salem

Old Salem Gardens
Off Route 52
Winston-Salem, NC 27108

Tel. (336) 721-7300
Open: (gardens) Mon.–Sat.
9:30–4:30; Sun. 1:30–4:30
Free: (gardens)

Old Salem is a restored late eighteenth- and early nineteenth-century community, originally settled by the Moravians. A visit to the town can include wonderful old period houses covering a 12-city-block area (call for details on hours and fees to visit the houses). Of particular interest to us are the many restored or recreated gardens, including several kitchen gardens, herb gardens, medicinal gardens, and even rose bushes planted in the early nineteenth century.

Old Salem (which puts out a brochure of garden descriptions available at the gate) has some 18 garden sites. The majority are kitchen gardens in fenced areas behind the houses. You'll find everything from perennial borders to fruit trees, beehives, vegetables, hops (for beer and bread), and a wide variety of herbs for cooking and medicinal use.

Not to be missed: Salt Street, where some of the most interesting gardens are to be found. The John Henry Leinbach property features a hilly garden that stretches down to a creek behind the house. (You can read his gardening diary at the site.) He terraced the land with a series of rock walls, planted potatoes and other vegetables, grew apples, and made honey, among many other gardening endeavors. His wife planted rosebushes in 1823 and they are still blooming atop the terrace. Also on Salt Street are gardens displaying medicinal herbs, a cherry orchard, and another garden of hops. Also, visit the Cape Fear Bank garden and the 1759 Triebel garden.

If you enjoy historic settings, with their antique ambiance, you will like these small, unpretentious Moravian plots with their combination of prettiness and usefulness. The people who have restored Old Salem have tried to retain the original atmosphere in each garden, and you can pretty well imagine yourself back in time, tending to the plantings.

Reynolda Gardens at Wake   *Tel. (336) 758-5593*
  Forest University   *Open: grounds, daily;*
100 Reynolda Village   *greenhouse, Mon.–Fri. 10–4*
Winston-Salem, NC 27106   *Free*

Reynolda Gardens, which cover 130 acres, were created more than 80 years ago by the noted Philadelphia architect Thomas Sears, for the R.J. Reynolds tobacco family. There are a variety of lovely garden features here, including four acres of meticulous, geometrically laid-out formal gardens, demonstration gardens, a three-section greenhouse, huge open lawns and meadows, and daffodil and log-lined nature trails through some 130 acres of woodlands, streams, ponds, and waterfalls. (You should take a map for the nature walk, since the trails are mostly unmarked.)

The great formal gardens are divided into Northern and Southern sections. A highlight is the All-American Rose Garden (visit in June or July), but there are many other attractions in these boxwood-edged, rectangular flowerbeds. A wisteria pergola, several arbors, and a reflecting pool accent the design. There are peonies, phlox, magnolias, flowering crab apples, weeping cherries in rows, and a group of stately Japanese cedars leading to The Lord and Burnham Greenhouse, a well cared-for facility used for research by the university, but open for the enjoyment of the public as well. Collections of orchids, bromeliads, and other tropical plantings are centerpieces of the collection within.

Over the near century of this garden's existence many of the trees and shrubs have grown so big that original designs for the formal gardens are sometimes no longer visible. But the resulting profusion of flowers and trees makes this combination of formal arrangements and natural landscape just right for a long walk (particularly as you get away from the traffic sounds) and there are beautifully placed, white painted benches surrounded by colonnades along the way.

SOUTH CAROLINA

Aiken
Charleston
Clemson
Columbia
Hartsville
Murrells Inlet
Orangeburg
Rock Hill
Spartanburg
Sumter

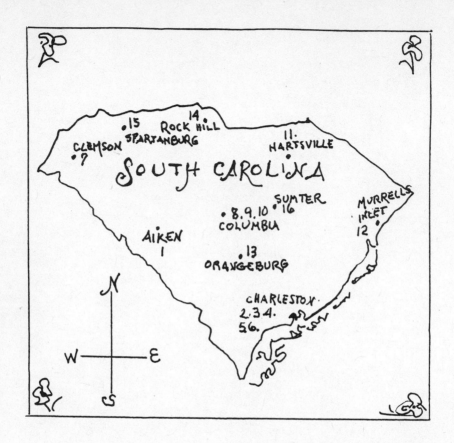

1. Aiken: Hopeland Gardens and Rye Patch
2. Charleston (Mt. Pleasant): Boone Hall Plantation
3. Charleston (Moncks Corner): Cypress Gardens
4. Charleston: Hampton Park
5. Charleston: Magnolia Plantation and Gardens
6. Charleston (Pinesville): Middleton Place
7. Clemson: South Carolina Botanical Garden
8. Columbia: Boylston Gardens
9. Columbia: Memorial Garden
10. Columbia: Robert Mills House
11. Hartsville: Kalmia Gardens of Coker College
12. Murrells Inlet: Brookgreen Gardens
13. Orangeburg: Edisto Memorial Gardens
14. Rock Hill: Glencairn Garden
15. Spartanburg: Hatcher Gardens
16. Sumter: Swan Lake Iris Gardens

⹂Aiken

Hopeland Gardens and Rye Patch
Whiskey Road and Mead Avenue
Aiken, SC 29802

Tel. (803) 642-7630
Open: daily, 10 A.M. to sunset
Free

It is always a pleasure to visit the 14-acre Hopeland Gardens, even on the hottest of summer days; for they are shaded by gazebos, willows, ancient live oaks, towering magnolias and deodar cedars, and cooled by fountains and pools. There are colorful blossoms to enjoy year-round as well, from fragrant spring roses, to crape myrtle blooms in summer, to camellias, azaleas, wisteria, magnolias, lilies, and dogwoods.

A scenic walk takes you past reflecting pools with statuary and fountains and two small lakes surrounded with weeping willows and spring bulbs. Other highlights at Hopeland include a Touch and Scent Trail for the visually impaired and the thoroughbred Racing Hall of Fame, appropriately located in what used to be a carriage house.

Hopeland Gardens and the adjoining estate, Rye Patch, were once the winter homes of the Iselin and Rogers families. Hope Goddard Iselin and her neighbor, Dorothy Knox Rogers, loved gardens and horses, passions which are reflected in both properties. Hopeland, the Iselin estate, is now a garden dotted with a few remaining structures (the house no longer exists). Among them are the carriage house and a very large doll house, now used as the Garden Club Council Center. The smaller property, Rye Patch, features the residence of the Rogers, as well as stables, a carriage house, and a memorial rose garden. When Mrs. Iselin died in 1970 (at age 102), her property was bequeathed to the city of Aiken and the gardens were redesigned for public use. In 1982 Rye Patch was also opened to the public.

Hopeland Gardens and Rye Patch are connected via meandering paths and a small footbridge over wetlands. Everything at both sites is free, except for a small fee to visit Rye Patch House, which will give you a taste of what life was once like for South Carolina's gentry.

Charleston

Boone Hall Plantation
P.O. Box 1554
Mt. Pleasant, SC 29465

Tel. (843) 884-4371
Open: April 1–Labor Day,
Mon.–Sat. 8:30–6:30 and
Sun. 1–5. Rest of the year,
Mon.–Sat. 9–5 and Sun. 1–4.
Closed Thanksgiving and
Christmas
Fee

With 738 acres of property, Boone Hall is a very grand plantation by any standard, but its most imposing feature by far (and well worth the price of admission alone) is its entrance, a half-mile live oak allée leading to the manor house. This is one of the fabled images of the Southern plantation that has been immortalized in everyone's imagination (it was the model for *Gone With the Wind*) and this particular avenue of ancient trees laced with dripping moss is the quintessential plantation sight.

The existing garden surrounding the plantation manor was designed early in the century. Among its delights are the graceful formal gardens of camellias and azaleas that surround brick walkways in front of the house, the variety of tulips and other spring bulbs scattered about the grounds, and the large collection of roses, some even centuries old, dating from the earliest settlement. A tour of the manor (a 1935 replica of the original eighteenth-century house), restored cotton gin houses, and nine remaining slave cabins (built in 1743 and listed in the National Register of Historic Places) is also highly recommended.

Boone Hall Plantation was named after Major John Boone, one of the original settlers of Charles Town in the late seventeenth century. At first a prosperous cotton plantation, it eventually became known for its hand-crafted bricks and tiles, which served many historic homes in the area. In the early part of this century the plantation also contained the world's largest pecan groves, many of which are still productive today.

Cypress Gardens
3030 Cypress Gardens Road
Moncks Corner, SC 29461

Tel. (843) 553-0515
Open: daily 9 to 5
Fee

Cypress Gardens is a mysterious forest of moss-covered cypress emerging from dark swamplands. The peaceful lakes, blackened by the acid from the trees, mirror the surrounding lush vegetation—thousands of azaleas and other flowering plants, not to mention the great trees themselves, standing in the smooth waters.

The 163 acres that now comprise the swamp gardens were once part of a riverside rice plantation endowed with natural lakes. In the late 1920s, years after the site had reverted to a wilderness, its owner, Benjamin Kittredge, decided to create a garden. An army of workers was hired to rid the lakes of debris; narcissus, wisteria, azaleas, daffodils, and lilies were planted along the shore; and paths were cleared deep into the forest. The gardens were opened to the public in 1963.

Today you can visit these atmospheric gardens on foot along three miles of woodsy footpaths or, for a fascinating glimpse into a world rarely seen from the shore, by flat-bottomed boat. The many horticultural offerings include the Azalea Garden, Camellia Garden, Woodland Garden, Butterfly Garden, and Garden of Memories. The best time to see the forest come alive with its thousands of bulbs and flowering plants is from February through the summer months.

Hampton Park　　　　　　　*Tel. (843) 724-7321*
30 Mary Murray Drive　　　 *Open: daily, dawn to dusk*
Charleston, SC 29403　　　 *Free*

This pretty city park, bordered by avenues of ancient oaks, is especially known for its formal rose walk. Here you can enjoy over 100 varieties of roses, along with groupings of camellias, azaleas, magnolias, crape myrtles, and many perennials. Also featured are a picturesque fountain and Victorian bandstand, where concerts are held during the summer.

Early in the century these grounds were part of a much larger tract of land slated to become a park designed by the Olmsted brothers of Boston. The illustrious plan was never realized, for half the property was given over to constructing The Citadel instead. Despite its reduced size, the existing 65-acre park is a spacious and pleasant place for a garden walk.

Magnolia Plantation and Gardens　*Tel. (843) 571-1266*
Route 61 (Ashley River Road)　　 *Open: daily 8–6*
Charleston, SC 29414　　　　　 *Fee*

Dating back to the 1680s, these are among America's oldest and most beautiful gardens, and among its most famous. Indeed, at the turn of the (twentieth) century they were even considered among its premier attractions, along with the Grand Canyon and Niagara Falls. Picturesquely set along the Ashley River about 10 miles from Charleston, and endowed with a magnificent landscape of ancient live oaks, tall cypress trees, haunting waterways, enchanting forests, and countless blossoms, they are the essence of the Southern plantation garden.

The present 50 acres of gardens, within a vast wildlife refuge, began in the seventeenth century as 10 acres of English-style flowerbeds and landscaped lawns. Over the years, under the care of successive family heirs (from the very beginning the site has been—and continues to be—owned and operated by the Drayton family), the gardens have grown and evolved into a more naturalistic mode. Lakes and pathways have been added, as have countless colorful plantings along the water, in forests, and in meadows.

The gardens combine romantic landscapes—dark pools reflecting lush vegetation, fields of wildflowers, enchanting waterside vistas—with more formal areas. Among the highlights are a camellia maze, a Biblical garden, a topiary garden featuring animals shaped from fig vines, an eighteenth-century herb garden, and the Barbados Tropical Garden, an enormous glass conservatory filled with exotic plants from the Drayton family's Caribbean origins.

If all these attractions weren't enough, there are still more: a 125-acre wildlife refuge (which can be enjoyed on foot or rented bike or canoe); an observation tower from which you can view 170 species of birds and waterfowl; and the nearby Audubon Swamp Garden, an atmospheric 60-acre tupelo and cypress swamp dotted with palmettos, wildflowers, and ferns, as well as herons, osprey, egrets, and even occasional alligators. (The site was named after John J. Audubon, who once came to visit the Draytons and study water birds.) Don't miss the plantation house, a historic landmark and museum featuring memorabilia and photos of early plantation life.

Magnolia Gardens are a wonder at any time of year. Bear in mind that the spring azaleas are among the best in the East. The rich camellia collection (over 900 varieties) is at its height between November and March; and summertime brings forth blooming hydrangeas, oleanders, roses, gardenias, crape myrtles, mimosas, and more.

Middleton Place　　　　　　　　　　*Tel. (843) 556-6020*
Ashley River Road　　　　　　　　　*Open: daily 9–5*
Charleston, SC 29414　　　　　　　*Fee*

Middleton Place is a celebration of nature at its most sublime. With its majestic vistas overlooking the serene Ashley River, its vast lawns and landscaped terraces, peaceful lakes, and magnificent old trees, this is truly a site not to be missed. Believed to be the oldest formal land-scaped garden in the country, Middleton Place reflects the grand symmetrical style of European gardens of the seventeenth and eighteenth centuries, particularly those of the French master, André Le Nôtre.

The gardens, arranged around a main axis in the French tradition, were laid out in 1741 by Henry Middleton, an influential social and political figure who eventually became president of the Continental Congress. For his magnificent estate he selected an unusually picturesque site along the shores of the Ashley River (where many other prominent Carolina families lived), on a bluff about 20 miles downstream of Charleston. The gardens, cut out of the tidewater wilderness, required the labors of 100 slaves for almost 10 uninterrupted years.

The landscape is a delight to explore at the leisurely pace that such an idyllic spot demands; you'll need plenty of time to contemplate the many views. Among the many sights to savor are the sculptured, gently undulating grass terraces descending gracefully to the water's edge; a pair of matching artificial lakes shaped like butterfly wings, separated by a grassy walkway; rectangular parterres of boxwood and crape myrtle surrounded by elegant walkways and shaded allées; and many, many blossoms that add charm to the Southern plantation ambiance, including azaleas, dogwoods, magnolias, and camellias, just to name a few. (The first four camellias in America were planted here in 1786; incredibly, three of these still exist, having grown to enormous size.)

One of the garden highlights is the "Middleton Oak," a magnificent 90-foot-tall specimen reputed to be a 1,000 years old. You will find it in a picture postcard setting overlooking the river. Other delights are the sunken octagonal garden, sundial garden, and two secret gardens that are enclosed, intimate, and perfect for a quiet conversation.

Now a designated National Historic Site, Middleton Place still includes traditional plantation features that give you a sense of what life was like here: farm yards, sugarcane works, stables, a blacksmith shop, even a few farm animals—cows and sheep that can be seen grazing on the vast front lawn. You can also visit the plantation house (the original one was burned to the ground during the Civil War, but the present one is still quite grand), which displays eighteenth- and nineteenth-century family furnishings and artifacts.

Clemson

South Carolina Botanical Garden
Clemson University/Perimeter
   Road
Dept. of Horticulture
P.O. Box 340375
Clemson, SC 29634

Tel. (864) 656-3405
Open: daily, dawn to dusk
Free

Located on the eastern side of Clemson University on land that was once the plantation of statesman John C. Calhoun, this garden has had several names. Originally known as the Horticultural Gardens of Clemson University, it later became the Clemson University Botanical Garden and, in 1992, the South Carolina Botanical Garden, the first botanical garden in the state.

Within these 270 leafy acres is a rich collection of plants, more than 2,000 varieties in all. In addition to the typical azaleas, rhododendrons, and camellias, there are a wildflower garden, bog and marsh habitat, fern garden, flower and turf garden, dwarf conifer garden, a Braille trail for the visually impaired, and a garden of meditation with picturesque glade, waterfalls, and pagoda. You will also find a demonstration vegetable and herb garden and pioneer complex, complete with log cabins, grist mill, and farm implements from colonial times.

The garden offers trails for hikers and bird watchers, guided nature walks, horticultural lectures, and a popular annual daffodil festival.

Columbia

Boylston Gardens
Governor's Mansion
800 Richland Street
Columbia, SC 29201

Tel. (803) 737-1710
Open: Mon.–Fri. 9:30–4:30
Free

These historic gardens are situated on a nine-acre site that includes three mansions dating from the mid-nineteenth century: the Governor's

Mansion, Caldwell-Boylston House, and Lace House. Recently restored, the gardens consist of elegant tree-lined paths leading to secluded areas; flowerbeds in colorful patterns; boxwood hedges; a rose garden; and statuary and fountains. There is also a brand-new and very popular wedding garden, which is as lovely as you might expect.

The original gardens, located behind Caldwell-Boylston House, were planted by Sarah Smith Boylston, a gifted horticulturist. At the end of World War II she donated a quarter-acre of her garden to the Garden Club of South Carolina to be dedicated as a memorial to those who fought and died. (See Memorial Garden, below.)

Although there is no fee to visit the gardens, you must make a reservation to tour the complex, allowing a good two hours to savor it all.

Memorial Garden　　　　　　　*Tel. (803) 796-6446*
Corner of Lincoln and　　　　　*Open: Sun. 1–5*
*　Calhoun Streets*　　　　　　　*Free*
Columbia, SC 29201

This tiny (quarter-acre) memorial garden provides an oasis of serenity within a lively, bustling city. An elaborate fence and imposing iron gates surround it completely, making it the appropriately peaceful sanctuary it is.

Once part of the adjacent Boylston Gardens (see above), it was dedicated in 1945 to commemorate those who fought and died during World War II. Developed by landscape designer Loutrel A. Briggs, it is an elegant combination of evergreens, star magnolias, dogwoods, camellias, and boxwoods.

If you decide to coordinate a visit to this tiny garden with the nearby Boylston Gardens, remember this garden is open for only a few hours on Sunday.

Robert Mills House　　　　　　*Tel. (803) 252-1770*
1616 Blanding Street　　　　　*Open: Grounds open daily,*
Columbia, SC 29201-3440　　　*dawn to dusk; house open*
　　　　　　　　　　　　　　Tues.–Sat. 10:15–3:15
　　　　　　　　　　　　　　No fee for the grounds
　　　　　　　　　　　　　　(fee for house tour)

This four-acre garden adorns one of Columbia's most beautiful historic houses. The Robert Mills House was named after the man who designed it in 1823, but was most famous for designing the Washington Monument. Originally a private home, it was later owned by the Presbyterian Church, and finally became a decorative arts museum in the 1960s.

The grounds showcase the Founder's Garden, a formal parterre of clipped boxwood hedges with roses, crape myrtles, native plants, and magnolia trees. Elegant urns and statuary are found amid the plantings. Beyond are broad expanses of lawn. Recently restored to its former glory, the garden is a graceful extension of one of several historic houses that is worth visiting in the Columbia area.

Hartsville

Kalmia Gardens of Coker College	*Tel. (843) 383-8145*
1624 West Carolina Avenue	*Open: daily, dawn to dusk*
Hartsville, SC 29550	*Free*

The mountain laurel ("Kalmia latifolia"), the featured plant here, gives the gardens its unusual name. Growing wild along the Black Creek, these white-blossomed shrubs are complemented by profusions of azaleas and camellias.

The 30-acre Kalmia Gardens are a naturalistic wonder of woodlands, streams, laurel thickets, and black swamp. You can stroll beneath the welcoming shade of pine, oak, and holly trees, and enjoy inviting walking trails, including the Camellia Trail, Bluff Trail, and Bog Garden Trail.

Located on a site that was once Laurel Land, the eighteenth-century plantation of Captain Thomas E. Hart, the gardens were developed during the 1930s, under the guidance of a determined lady named May Roper Coker. "Miss May's Folly," as the project was described by some skeptics during those difficult Depression years, opened its doors to the public in 1935. (Miss May has been more than vindicated since then, with the resulting woodland paradise.) Finally, in the mid-1960s the gardens were donated to Coker College.

Although open year-round, Kalmia Gardens are especially spectacular during May, when the mountain laurels are in full bloom.

Murrells Inlet

Brookgreen Gardens
1931 Brookgreen Gardens Drive
Highway 17S
Pawley's Island, SC 29585

Tel. (843) 235-6000
Open: daily 9:30–4:45
Fee

"Brookgreen Gardens is a quiet joining of hands between science and art . . . " With these words, Archer M. Huntington, who created this site in 1931 with his wife, noted sculptor Anna Hyatt Huntington, described the mission of the gardens. The land surrounding their home was not only to be an outdoor gallery for the works of great sculptors (including Mrs. Huntington herself), but also to be a nature sanctuary—to perpetuate its natural beauty and provide a safe haven for its wildlife. In fact, Brookgreen is a remarkable 300-acre garden with sculpture, as well as plants, surrounded by a 9,000-acre preserve.

The art collection contains about 550 works by some 250 noted sculptors, largely American, magnificently set amid terraces, pools, fountains, and the lush plantings typical of the region. Here you will see works by such artists as Frederic Remington, Carl Milles, Daniel Chester French, and Paul Manship, not to mention Anna Hyatt Huntington.

But the gardens are hardly secondary to the art and are well worth a visit in their own right. Anna Hyatt Huntington was not only a highly regarded sculptor (among her works on display is her "Fighting Stallions," the largest sculpture ever cast in aluminum), but also a masterful gardener. She herself drew up the basic garden design for Brookgreen. A beautiful 250-year-old live oak allée leads to connecting informal gardens whose pathways wind around in the shape of an enormous butterfly. The gardens are planted with azaleas, dogwoods, magnolias, and other flowering varieties that create vibrant color, especially in spring. In addition, some 2,000 native wildflowers and plants add their natural beauty to the grounds.

Nature lovers won't want to miss the wildlife park, adjacent to the sculpture gardens. Included are a walk-through cypress and bird sanctuary, otter pond, alligator swamp, fox and raccoon glade, deer savannah, and other delights.

Orangeburg

Edisto Memorial Gardens　　　*Tel. (803) 534-6376*
Highway 301 South　　　　　*Open: daily, dawn to dusk*
Orangeburg, SC 29115　　　　*Free*

It is easy to understand why Edisto Memorial Gardens receives so many visitors each year. Idyllically set along the Edisto River, the longest black water river in the world, it combines rich plantings of azaleas, dogwoods, and roses with majestic and towering oaks and cypress trees.

The gardens—presently over 150 acres, including a recently added six-acre wetlands accessible by boardwalk—began modestly as a small city park with a few azaleas plantings. In 1951 a rose garden was added; it is now a major highlight of the garden. Endowed with over 50 beds and featuring more than 4,000 roses, from miniatures to tall, climbing specimens, this specialty garden has been designated an All-American Rose Selections display garden. Each year, during the last week of April, it is featured in the South Carolina Festival of Roses.

On the grounds there is also a fountain commemorating the soldiers who died in these last wars, giving the garden its name.

Rock Hill

Glencairn Garden　　　　　*Tel. (803) 329-5620*
Edgemont Avenue　　　　　*Open: daily, dawn to dusk*
Rock Hill, SC 29731　　　　 *Free*

Azaleas—thousands of them—and flowering trees abound on these lush grounds. From mid- to late April especially, the many magnolias, dogwoods, redbuds, crape myrtles, daffodils, and wisteria are a sight to see. They are the main draw for Rock Hill's weeklong "Come See Me" festival.

Once private (it was named after the owners' ancestral home in Scotland), Glencairn was opened to the public in 1940. This formal seven-and-a-half-acre garden is a harmonious combination of terraced lawns, a fountain gently cascading down stone tiers to a lily pond, a Japanese footbridge, and flowerbeds of summer annuals. Winding paths meander throughout, past the colorful banks of azaleas, grape hyacinths, and other garden delights.

Besides strolling and nature watching, Glencairn also provides a romantic setting for art shows, concerts and, of course, weddings.

Spartanburg

Hatcher Gardens
820 Reidville Road
Spartanburg, SC 29302

Tel. (864) 582-0138
Open: daily 9 A.M. to dusk
Free

Harold Hatcher created this naturalistic seven-acre garden that bears his name. In 1969 he began to transform an overgrown urban eyesore into a lush garden. Gradually acquiring more property, he and his wife almost single-handedly cleared and reshaped the landscape, and planted thousands of native varieties. In the late 1980s they donated this sanctuary to the city, so that others could learn more about plants and be inspired to preserve the environment.

The garden is an inviting landscape of tall trees, shrubs, wildflowers, picturesque ponds, and wildlife. Some of the plantings you will likely spot (from an observation deck or walking trails) are red buckeye, witch hazel, pawpaw, magnolia, jack-in-the-pulpit, deutzia, beauty bush, winter Daphne, and Virginia bluebell. Blossom season is from early spring to late fall, so plan accordingly.

Sumter

Swan Lake Iris Gardens
822 West Liberty Street
Sumter, SC 29151

Tel. (800) 688-4748
Open: daily, dawn to dusk
Free

This dream garden could be straight out of an Impressionist painting. The scene shows a peaceful lake dotted with little islands, black and white swans, water lilies, and lotuses. The dark waters reflect the colors of the surrounding foliage—pale pinks, creamy yellows, soft lavenders, and deep, deep purples. Masses of azaleas, camellias, magnolias, wisteria, and—most notably—iris are framed by towering oaks and cypress.

The incredible Japanese iris collection shares center stage with the eight species of swans (gathered from around the world) that float languidly amid lily pads and wander about the gardens. There are millions of irises (apparently six million!) in a rainbow of colors, an unforgettable sight during blooming season in May.

The gardens began in a serendipitous fashion. When Hamilton Carr Bland, a local businessman and amateur gardener, was unsuccessful in growing irises in his own backyard, he disposed of the uprooted flowers, carelessly tossing them on the banks of a nearby swamp. Unexpectedly, the plants thrived there, indicating to him that these wetlands were the ideal site for the iris garden he had always wanted. With the addition of a large piece of wooded land and much imaginative planting, Swan Lake Iris Gardens were launched. In the late 1940s they were opened to an enthusiastic public.

Since then the 150-acre gardens have been embellished with more landscaped areas, lawns, rustic bridges, and shaded pathways. To make the site even more pleasurable to families, park amenities such as picnic tables and tennis courts have also been added.

TENNESSEE

Chattanooga

Hermitage

Knoxville

Memphis

Nashville

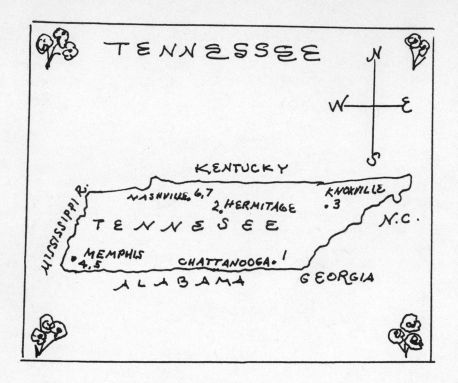

1. Chattanooga: Reflection Riding
2. Hermitage: The Hermitage
3. Knoxville: Blount Mansion
4. Memphis: Memphis Botanic Garden
5. Memphis: Dixon Gallery and Gardens
6. Nashville: Cheekwood
7. Nashville: Opryland

Chattanooga

Reflection Riding
Chattanooga Nature Center
Route 4/400 Garden Road
Chattanooga, TN 37419

Tel. (423) 821-9582
Open: Mon.–Sat. 9–5; Sun. 1–5
Fee

This vast 300-acre nature preserve/botanical garden is yet another reason to visit Chattanooga, a city known for its Civil War battlefields and many museums. At Reflection Riding, you can view, on foot or from your car, a wide variety of wildflowers set amidst flowering shrubs and trees, reminiscent of a romantic English landscape. Vividly colorful azaleas, rhododendrons, asters, mountain laurels, and other plantings can be enjoyed from spring into autumn, although the park is open in the winter, too. A nature center offers educational programs, workshops, and displays geared to all ages.

Hermitage

The Hermitage
4580 Rachel's Lane
Hermitage, TN 37076

Tel. (615) 889-2941
Open: daily 9–5, except third
  week of January; Thanksgiving, and Christmas
Fee

Here is a small garden, only one acre in all, but an historically important site 12 miles east of Nashville. Set within the vast and hilly 625-acre estate of President Andrew Jackson, it is known as "Rachel's Garden." His wife, Rachel Jackson, was in fact an avid amateur horticulturist—a visitor to the Jackson home once remarked he had never met anyone who loved flowers as much as she. And after she died in 1828, her devoted husband not only had her buried there amidst her beloved flowers, but took special care that the garden would always be perfectly maintained in her memory.

Some years after buying this property in 1804, the Jacksons decided to create a residence more in keeping with their increasing national prominence (they had been living in a small log cabin on the premises). Apparently they were inspired by such elegant Virginia plantations as Mount Vernon. They engaged a well-regarded Philadel-

147

phia landscape designer, William Frost, for the grounds. Rachel worked closely with him in designing the small formal garden right next to the mansion and, until her premature death 10 years later, helped maintain it.

Even though the garden was always considered an integral part of the quite grand estate, it was not, and is not, pretentious (though today's garden may be a bit fancier and more manicured than the original). English in style, it includes a group of rectangular and circular flowerbeds at the center, contained by unusual bricks and pebbled pathways. Surrounding them are four large grassy squares bordered with flowers and herbs. (During the time of the Jacksons there was also an abundance of vegetables.) Among the many varieties of flowering plants are hickory and magnolia trees planted during the Jacksons' lifetime. The garden is now enclosed by a white picket fence.

The Ladies' Hermitage Association, which took over the upkeep of the property in the late 1880s and maintains it impeccably to this day, has restored much of Rachel's Garden over the years. Although the plantings today are purely ornamental, except for a few herbs, and do not include Jackson's much loved vegetables, they reflect the love and care of flowers that were essential to Rachel.

Knoxville

Blount Mansion
200 W. Hill Avenue
Knoxville, TN 37901

Tel. (423) 525-2375
Open: April–Nov., Tues.–Sat. 10–5
and Sun. 1–5; winter months,
Tues.–Fri. 10–5
Fee

Surrounding a late eighteenth-century manor house is this colorful colonial-style garden. The garden may remind you of some at Colonial Williamsburg. In fact, it was redesigned in 1960 by landscape architects from that historic site. An unusually long boxwood walkway sets off formal beds of wildflowers, annuals, perennials, and herbs. In spring it is featured as part of the area's annual Dogwood Arts Festival.

History buffs will also want to visit the 1792 frame house, locally referred to as the "mansion," a Registered National Historic Landmark. It was here that William Blount (governor of the territory south of the Ohio River and a delegate to the Federal Constitutional Convention) and his associates planned the admission of Tennessee as the nation's 16th state in 1796.

ℳℯ𝓂𝓅𝒽𝒾𝓈

Memphis Botanic Garden
750 Cherry Road
Memphis, TN 38117

Tel. (901) 685-1566
Open: Nov.–Feb., Mon.–Sat.
 9–4:30 and Sun. 11–4;
 March–Oct., Mon.–Sat. 9–6
 and Sun. 11–6
Fee

Within this flower-loving, green city of urban parks and garden areas is the 87-acre Memphis Botanic Garden, famous for its lovely and extensive displays. Among its many offerings are a four-acre Japanese garden surrounding Lake Biwa (stocked with thousands of goldfish!), the outstanding seven-acre Ketchum Memorial Iris Garden with hundreds of varieties that bloom over a six-week period, and a 10-acre arboretum containing an impressive collection of domestic and foreign shrubs and trees. You'll also find an extensive Wildflower Garden, a daffodil collection, a lovely rose garden with more than 3,000 bushes, an azalea trail of brilliant colors, and a fern glen. There are also gardens of daylilies, dahlias, and magnolias.

A conservatory contains noteworthy tropical plant collections, a camellia house, and seasonal displays. In the Garden Center is an elegant courtyard water garden. Oriental in style, it features fountains trickling into a reflecting pool bordered by evergreens. The Center also contains a library, gift shop, and meeting rooms for educational programs, garden clubs, and plant societies.

Dixon Gallery and Gardens
4339 Park Avenue
Memphis, TN 38117

Tel. (901) 761-2409
Open: Tues.–Sat. 10–5; Sun., 1–5
Fee

Just minutes from Memphis's lively downtown you'll discover a delightful oasis of shade, tranquillity, and quiet beauty. Dixon Gallery and Gardens offers naturalistic woodlands, a collection of carefully designed formal, intimate gardens, and grassy terraces with vistas in an English parklike landscape. Once the private estate of Margaret and Hugo Dixon—she was from Mississippi, he from England, and they shared a great love of nature—it includes a 17-acre garden surrounding an elegant Georgian house, now a gallery of Impressionist and Post-Impressionist painting.

The Dixons, who had traveled around the country and throughout Europe visiting gardens, bought a small untamed property in 1939 (it was much expanded as the years went by) and, with the help of Hugo's sister, Hope Crutchfield, began to design the grounds. Fortunately, they carefully preserved most of the majestic old trees that give the garden its cathedral-like aura, not to mention its particularly inviting shaded walkways. Beneath stately canopies of oaks and hickories they added to the indigenous dogwoods and hemlocks and planted azaleas and boxwood. Connecting garden rooms feature colorful flowerbeds that provide visual interest year-round.

The gardens are landscaped around two main axes: the north-south axis includes the house at one end and an impressive sculpture of Europa and the Bull at the other; the east-west axis, an elegant avenue of azaleas and evergreens, is called the "Venus allée" for its 1960s statue of Venus at one end. (A swimming pool is at the other end.)

Brick paths lead to a group of formal gardens graced with an abundance of flowers. (Mrs. Dixon chose to have white flowers next to the house, with bright colors beyond.)

You won't want to miss the extraordinary camellia collection. More than 200 plants are on display in an enclosed setting, from November to March (remember that February is the peak month for camellias). Behind the camellia house is a charming cutting garden, featuring narcissus and tulips in spring, and phlox, hydrangeas, daisies, and other old-fashioned blossoms in summer. Throughout the garden you'll find small park benches, carefully framed with wildflowers or ferns or mosses.

Dixon Gardens is especially lovely in spring, when its multitude of azaleas and wildflowers are truly breathtaking. But this is a place for all seasons, offering visual pleasure throughout the year.

Nashville

Cheekwood
1200 Forrest Park Drive
Nashville, TN 37205

Tel. (615) 353-2148
Open: Mon.–Sat. 9–5; Sun. 11–5,
except holidays
Fee

With its imposing hilltop Georgian-style mansion surrounded by handsome gardens and grounds, Cheekwood is reminiscent of a grand, English estate. In fact, it was the home of Leslie and Mabel Cheek, who had a particular fondness for eighteenth-century-style English houses and gardens. They had visited a number of traditional country estates during their frequent travels abroad in the 1920s, and inspired by these, they created Cheekwood on their newly purchased property just southwest of Nashville.

Today this 55-acre site is a combination botanical garden and fine-arts museum (in the 1950s the then owners donated the house and about half of their land for this cultural purpose).

The splendid grounds offer a wide range of gardens, both formal and woodsy, from the English flower gardens and boxwood hedges designed by the Cheeks and their gardeners to more recent additions. You'll find a Japanese tea garden complete with bamboo gate, dry streambed of pebbles and dwarf conifers; a scent and taste garden for the visually impaired; a trillium collection, reputed to be the largest of its kind in the Southeast; a fine iris collection (particularly apt, since the iris is Tennessee's state flower); and daffodil, herb, rose, and peony gardens. Along woodland paths are azaleas, dogwoods, and wildflowers, all spectacular in spring. And you can enjoy garden statuary, ponds, fountains, and broad vistas throughout the gardens and from the house and surrounding hillside.

Adding to these pleasures are greenhouses featuring orchids, camellias, and species native to the cloud forests of Central America. Next to the mansion is a romantic wrought-iron arbor of wisterias, as well as reflecting pools (with water lilies in summer), fountains, and some of the earliest of the boxwood collection.

Don't miss the Cheek house itself, with its permanent collection of nineteenth- and twentieth-century American artists and special exhibits.

Opryland USA　　　　　　　　*Tel. (615) 889-1000*
2800 Opryland Drive　　　　　*Open: daily, at all times*
Nashville, TN 37214　　　　　*Free*

The name "Opryland" brings to mind country western music and other lively entertainments. But gardens? In fact, surprisingly, within the enormous resort called the Opryland Hotel are three indoor conservatory gardens that are quite remarkable and well worth a visit.

Occupying several acres (requiring a longish walk), they feature winding walkways perched high above dramatic botanic displays. Hundreds of tropical and subtropical plants—brilliant flowers and exotic trees—are set amidst ravines, rocky coves, waterfalls, fountains, and terraces. One of these glass-roofed gardens, perhaps the boldest and most Disneyesque in concept, includes three massive waterfalls spilling down an artificial 40-foot "mountain" surrounded by thousands of brightly colored plants.

This fanciful slice of botanic Americana should engage just about anyone, from young children to serious garden lovers to foreign visitors. The gardens at Opryland are, in fact, an entertainment as well as a "garden experience."

VIRGINIA

Alexandria   Arrington
Boyce   Charles City
Charlottesville   Clarksville
Fredericksburg   Harrisonburg
Leesburg   Lorton
Manassas   Montpelier
Mount Vernon   Norfolk
Richmond   Staunton
Stratford   Surry
Virginia Beach   Williamsburg

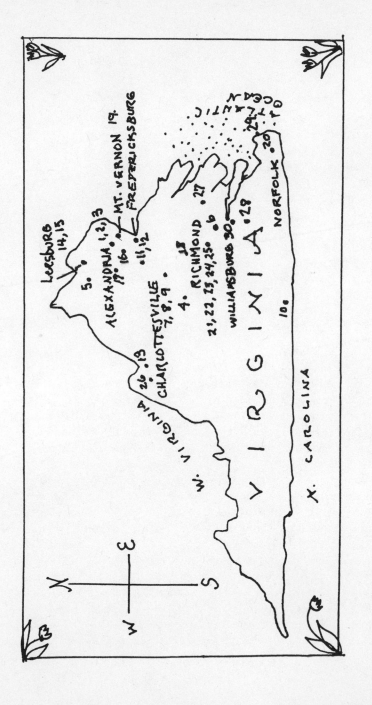

Alexandria

Green Spring Gardens Park
4603 Green Springs Road
Alexandria, VA 22312

Tel. (703) 642-5173
Open: daily, dawn to dusk
Free

No less than two dozen different gardens are presented on this 27-acre former farm with an eighteenth-century manor house. Horticulture is taken seriously here; there is a greenhouse as well as many classes, research facilities, and garden events. The gardens themselves, which are comparatively new, surround a large circular lawn. No matter what your horticultural interests are, you are sure to find a garden to capture your attention: a butterfly garden, an iris garden, a garden of everlastings for making dried flower arrangements, a boxwood garden, a dye garden, a rose garden, a witch hazel collection, a blue garden, and a native plant and pond area. Visit at any time of year; there is always something growing.

River Farm
7931 East Boulevard Drive
Alexandria, VA 22308

Tel. (800) 777-7931
Open: May 1–Oct. 30, Mon.–Fri.
8:30–5; some weekends
Fee

George Washington purchased this farm above the Potomac River (and just minutes away from Mount Vernon) in 1760. Though he never lived on the farm, he planted wheat, rye, and corn, and is thought to have planted the walnut trees in the meadow. Now the headquarters for the American Horticultural Society, it naturally has extensive and very pretty gardens.

River Farm is at the top of a hill overlooking the Potomac and its curious meandering shores. There are a large elegant house and a series of garden areas, including various types of gardens—as befits a horticultural society. You'll find many kinds of garden settings, ranging from an America's Front Yard Garden, a Children's Garden, a Wildlife Garden, and even that English necessity, a ha-ha wall, to the more traditional rose garden and perennial plantings. Many are trial gardens run by the Society; the dahlia beds are one of seven such trial sites in the nation, and there are over 100 types of daylilies in another spot. Some of the garden features go quite far back in history. The boxwood hedges, for example, were planted in Lincoln's time.

Each of the display gardens is extensive and very luxuriant in season, and obviously well worth visiting, for these gardeners are definitely experts. The herb garden, for instance, was designed by a specialist from the United States Botanic Garden. It has herbs for aromatherapy, flavor, habitat, and health, surrounded by various unusual trees, like the silver weeping peach. Spring shrubs are also well represented here. The dogwood collection has many rare species, as does the azalea garden (which is maintained by the Azalea Society of America). Both gardens are particularly dazzling in April and May. The garden for children is a particular pleasure, and we recommend it. There is a bat cave, an alphabet garden, and even a garden that displays all the ingredients found on the average pizza! Kids will love this spot.

For the traditionalist, the flower-filled spaces behind the house are very lovely. Under a series of brick arches, and surrounded by brick walls, these beds include All-American selections (labeled) of every kind of bloom beloved by home gardeners.

Woodlawn Plantation　　　　　　*Tel. (703) 780-4000*
9000 Richmond Highway　　　　*Open: Mon.–Sat. 10–4; Sun. 1–4*
Alexandria, VA 22309　　　　　 *Fee*

This pretty estate overlooking the Potomac was given by George Washington to his step-granddaughter Nelly as a wedding present. The fine house was designed by Dr. William Thornton, the first architect of the United States Capitol. Unfortunately, Woodlawn and its land (originally 2,000 acres) had a checkered history through the nineteenth and twentieth centuries, including serious storm damage, tree cutting, subdividing, and near decay and ruin (some 60 cats lived there at one time). In 1951 the National Trust took charge, and today there are 20 acres of restored gardens, with a particular emphasis on parterre gardens with boxwood hedges and roses. If rose gardens are your special interest don't miss Woodlawn. The gardens border an irregular lawn with informal clusters of trees and shrubs. The restoration has been accomplished using old descriptions and records as much as possible. Visit in late spring and early summer.

Arrington

Oak Ridge Estate
2300 Oak Ridge Road
Arrington, VA 22922

Tel. (804) 263-8676
Open: summer, Tues.–Thurs.
10–3, or phone for additional
times
Fee

We approached Oak Ridge on a narrow drive through what seemed miles of picturesque rural scenery. In fact, a lot of it belongs to this amazing estate of some 4,000 acres. When we finally reached the fine white mansion and gardens, we were struck by the overwhelming sense of the past. Everything about Oak Ridge is old, and a lot of it somewhat decayed—in the nicest sense. A reconstruction is taking place, and we can only hope that the current owners retain the evocative air of faded elegance and eccentricity.

If your idea of a plantation estate is a spiffy reconstruction complete with costumed docents, this is not the place for you. On the other hand, if you respond to a decidedly Southern ambiance with a grand old mansion set in a lovely green landscape with great oak trees (one is 350 years old), winding paths, the haunting, grass-filled skeleton of a conservatory, and ancient statues and overgrown gardens, this is certainly the place to come. The sweeping panorama of Oak Ridge is a taste of the Deep South in rural Virginia, only a short drive from sophisticated Charlottesville. Unlike most Southern open-to-the-public plantations, its major period of elegance came well after the antebellum period.

The original estate dates to the eighteenth century. The mansion was constructed in 1802—influenced by Thomas Jefferson's designs— by a tobacco planter named Robert Rives. Its owners included his unmarried daughter, who successfully ran the plantation herself, and a number of notable Virginians, including a Confederate congressman. When Thomas Fortune Ryan took possession in 1901, Oak Ridge's glory days began. Ryan, a Virginian who was a poor orphan as a child, became one of the nation's richest men, and Oak Ridge was to become his showplace, his own personal city. Like the Vanderbilts in New York, Ryan traveled about on his own train car. One of the delights of this visit is seeing his private station and the tracks and gilded railroad gate that bisect his vast property. Don't fail to walk down through the sloping grounds to this piece of Americana, and to visit the iron-fenced gravesites.

Ryan employed some 300 people at Oak Ridge, among them a legion of gardeners, lawn keepers, beekeepers, and an estate florist. He had the once-elegant Italianate formal gardens installed and a large rose garden put in. The great conservatory, modeled after the famous domed greenhouse in the Crystal Palace in England, was built near the house. Today you can see the structure in its evocative ruined state. Behind the mansion the formal gardens are terraced and outlined in boxwood. There are statues and ornaments and an old well cover adorning the gardens and accenting the geometric patterns of the plantings. Some of the statues are purported to be from the Renaissance. There is also an artistic waterfall designed by Mrs. Ryan and called "Crabtree Falls Cascade." At Oak Ridge, the gentle decay and ancient trees seem like metaphors for the passage of time.

Boyce

Orland E. White Arboretum
U.S. Route 50
Boyce, VA 22620

Tel. (540) 837-1758
Open: daily, dawn to dusk
Free

This is a most unusual arboretum, with a specialty of boxwood. In fact, this is the largest collection of boxwood in the nation. The arboretum also features fully half of the world's pine species and a grove of 350 ginkgo trees. As for gardens, you'll find a native Virginia plant trail, and collections of azaleas, perennials, daylilies, and herbs. You can walk here, or take a three-mile driving loop.

Charles City

Berkeley Plantation
12602 Harrison Landing
Road (Route 5)
Charles City, VA 23030

Tel. (804) 829-6018
Open: daily 8–5
Fee

This is the quintessential James River plantation to visit. It has history, charm, and lovely gardens. Berkeley was the home that Benjamin Harrison IV and his wife, Anne, built in 1726. The Georgian mansion is said to be the oldest three-story brick house in Virginia. The plantation can boast of many historical highlights. It was the site of the first

Thanksgiving in America and the birthplace of a signer of the Declaration of Independence, as well as of the ninth president of the United States, William Henry Harrison. George Washington and nine succeeding Presidents visited the plantation. Berkeley was the site of a Civil War encampment of some 140,000 Northern troops, reviewed by President Lincoln in 1862. ("Taps" was written there at the same time.) It might also be noted that the first Bourbon in America was distilled at Berkeley.

With such an illustrious history, it is no wonder that Berkeley is a much-visited site. Its gardens are among its notable attractions. Formal, terraced, boxwood gardens interspersed with flowers, and a large green lawn cover 10 acres, extending a quarter of a mile down to the banks of the James River. A charming gazebo, known as the Tea and Mint Julep House, ornaments the landscape. Great trees surround the house. If you are at nearby Williamsburg, this is an easy detour to make, and certainly a pleasant one.

Charlottesville

Ash Lawn-Highland
James Monroe Parkway
Charlottesville, VA 22902

Tel. (804) 293-9539
Open: Mar. to Oct., 9–6; Nov.
to Feb., 10–5
Fee

This very pretty estate was the home of President James Monroe from 1799 to 1823. Monroe built the Charlottesville house so as to be close to Jefferson at Monticello (and you will find visiting both gardens convenient as well). The house and gardens have been tastefully restored. This garden will particularly interest those with a taste for old-fashioned boxwood gardens; these are filled with specimen plants and they bloom profusely throughout a long season. There is also a fine herb garden, and you may find peacocks strolling through the scenic landscape.

Monticello
Route 53 (P.O. Box 316)
Charlottesville, VA 22901

Tel. (804) 984-9822
Open: Nov.–Feb., daily 9–4:30;
Mar.–Oct., 8–5
Fee

Every inch of this beautiful place built and landscaped by Thomas Jefferson is so deeply connected with history and significance that it's hard to separate and describe just the gardens. In fact, if your only interest is flower gardens per se, you'll have to block out a fascinating collection of extraneous material on your tour, for each corner of Monticello has something to capture your attention. Monticello is one of the nation's most worthy and delightful historic estates, the physical representation of Jefferson's genius. He was a gardener par excellence, as well as an architect and statesman, and here at Monticello you'll find many of his ideas about gardens and nature and economy that were put into practice in the early nineteenth century.

The gardens have been elegantly restored by the Garden Club of Virginia (using Jefferson's own notes and drawings and correspondence); they were an abiding interest of the President's. "No occupation," he wrote, "is so delightful to me as the culture of the earth, and no culture comparable to that of the garden. . . . But though an old man, I am but a young gardener."

There are two miles of trails throughout this 95-acre estate. They skirt three lakes, hills, forest, orchards, and flower gardens. Along the walk are seasonal plantings and flowering trees of all types. The flower gardens themselves are at the four corners of the house. Twenty oval-shaped beds with a winding gravel walk through them are especially pretty in spring and early summer. The serpentine walk and surrounding lawn are bordered with flowers, and everything is labeled. Among the great varieties of blooms here are not just the familiar spring bulbs, but such rarities as a Jeffersonia diphylla (named, of course, for the master) and a Columbian lily (a discovery of Lewis and Clark).

Among the interesting sights are a 1,000-foot-long terraced vegetable garden, which features delightful patterns and climbing varieties, including some of the 20 types of peas Jefferson grew—peas were apparently Jefferson's favorite vegetable. He grew over 250 types of vegetables and herbs here. The garden, which is divided into 27 growing beds, has a stone wall with a reconstructed pavilion where Jefferson sat to read among the vegetables. There is a research facility at Monticello that studies propagation and historic plants. You can also purchase historic seeds.

To appreciate fully the grand plan of Monticello's gardens requires understanding Jefferson's goals and preoccupations (and the tour center, guides, and printed material are fully prepared to help you). But you can also walk around and enjoy this elegant and historic site with a minimum of knowledge and the greatest of aesthetic pleasure.

Pavilion Gardens   *Tel. (804) 924-7969*
University of Virginia   *Open: daylight hours*
Charlottesville, VA 22903   *Free*

Thomas Jefferson's campus at the university here is a graceful, green wonder. Its beautifully aged brick walls and white pillars harmonize completely with the landscape. In addition to the architectural delights set amid the lovely landscape with its grand, imposing trees, are the pavilion gardens that the master statesman, architect, and gardener included in his plan. Though Jefferson did not himself lay out each of these 10 gardens, his original design included the serpentine garden walls and the concept of the individual gardens in conjunction with the groves of academe. The pavilions are behind each of the old brick houses; their object was to provide a place for contemplation and study for members of the "academic village."

You can take a formal tour or pick up a brochure describing each pavilion garden, walking unescorted from one to the next, through little white connecting doors here and there. The high walls provide a privacy that makes each entrance to a garden a new experience. The gardens are divided into two sections matching the two facing rows of arcades that border the great lawn and the Rotunda. Behind these original buildings you'll find the five East Pavilion Gardens and the five West Pavilion Gardens. Each is different; those on the west side are predominantly flat, while the east gardens are hilly and terraced. The overall sense of each of the gardens is of Jefferson's time, and a variety of experts have managed to recreate the eighteenth-century era in both the geometric designs and the plantings.

If you begin your walk on the west side with Pavilion Garden I, you'll find a geometrically patterned garden with a serpentine walk reflecting the curving walls and small oval flowerbeds. A center stone was an attempt by Jefferson to carve capitols for the Rotunda from local stone. Pavilion Garden III, next door, has raised oval flowerbeds and unusually pretty trees, among them a silverbell and a goldenrain. Next door in Garden V are two of Jefferson's favorite apple trees, set in the center of a series of squares with parterres and gravel walks. This garden is divided into upper and lower sections; the higher part includes a formal boxwood garden and lovely crape myrtle trees. Garden VII is characterized by benches along curving walks bordered by roses. Garden IX also has a two-part design; its lower part is cool and shady with large trees and pomegranate shrubs, while the upper garden features a four-part formal arrangement of viburnum, peonies, and lilacs. On the east side of the great lawn is Pavilion Garden II, which is divided into three sections, with great trees, including an umbrella magnolia and a pecan tree, as well as a grape arbor and many fruit trees. Next door in Garden IV there is a combination of formality in a boxwood garden and informal flowerbeds in natural settings. Garden VI is one of the best known; here the Merton Spire (given by Oxford University) is in the center of a naturalistic rhododendron and laurel garden. Garden VIII is a summer garden, with profusely blooming shrubs and an "aerial hedge" of goldenrain trees. The final, and one of the largest, is Garden X. Its design is actually based on the Monticello gardens, with an oval lawn flanked by two smaller ovals (called elephant ears) and a romantic setting of benches amid Kentucky coffee trees. These thumbnail descriptions cannot begin to describe the atmosphere in these gardens, particularly in springtime. You'll seldom see prettier or more historic campus gardens.

Clarksville

Prestwould Plantation
U.S. Highway 15 (east of
*   Clarksville)*
Clarksville, VA 23927

Tel. (804) 374-8672
Open: daily 1:30–4:30
Fee

One of the most interesting things about a visit here is that you can see both the reconstructed gardens and the model of the original garden, on display in the octagonal summer house. The Prestwould house was built in 1795. The gardens—outlined with original ancient boxwoods that are as much as 30 feet in diameter—are described as an Interpretative Restoration based on detailed plans and extensive records made by Lady Jean Skipwith. She was the wife of Sir Peyton Skipwith—the only baron born in Virginia—who won the 10,000-acre estate gambling with William Byrd III of Westover. In any case, Lady Jean was a great gardener, and her records, kept over a 20-year period, are among the earliest known listings of native plantings; Lady Jean is considered the most important woman gardener in eighteenth- or early nineteenth-century America.

The setting of Prestwould's gardens was an unusual one, a virtual island between two rivers. The house was on the hilly terrain above, with well-landscaped grounds sloping down to the river. Lady Skipwith's garden included orchards and native wildflowers that could be seen from the house on the hill. She combined agriculture and landscape design in an unusually sophisticated fashion. She also relished the native plants of the Virginia wilderness, describing her island garden as "a cabinet of curiosities." The reconstruction has followed her notes as faithfully as possible, both in the plantings and the trellises and arbors of the charming setting. If your interests tend toward early American garden design and indigenous plants, as well as lovely garden vistas, this visit should capture your imagination.

Fredericksburg

Kenmore
1201 Washington Avenue
Fredericksburg, VA 22401

Tel. (540) 373-3381
Open: Mar.–Nov., daily 9–5;
closed certain holidays
Fee for house visit, free for gardens

It is not surprising that many visitors are particularly drawn to Kenmore, one of the many historic houses that grace the region. A picture-perfect eighteenth-century estate set on four acres of broad lawns, with gardens and stately trees, it combines classic simplicity with a touch of formality. The Georgian manor, whose unpretentious façade belies an elaborate interior of magnificently decorated rooms—some consider it to be among the most beautiful period rooms in America— was built in the mid-eighteenth century by Colonel Fielding Lewis, George Washington's brother-in-law. Washington, a frequent visitor, is reported to have designed some of the ornate interior plasterwork himself. The house was surrounded by a 13,000-acre plantation; today, just five acres of gardens remain, but what lovely, serene gardens they are!

Kenmore's restoration began in the 1920s, after a somewhat turbulent history, including war and inevitable neglect. In 1929 the Garden Club of Virginia decided it was high time to do something about the unkempt grounds. To accomplish a full-scale renovation, they initiated Historic Garden Week, a fundraising event that has since benefited many other gardens throughout the South. Mindful of the historic significance of the estate, they introduced plantings in keeping with its setting and period.

Today the gardens (which have undergone yet another renovation) are a harmonious blend of graceful formality and natural beauty. Within the grounds are restful expanses of grass shaded by venerable hardwood trees, a wilderness area laced with wildflowers, and many beautifully tended plantings. Among the specialties are a colorful cutting garden and many flowering trees and shrubs, including rhododendrons, boxwoods, camellias, and dogwoods. A magical time to visit Kenmore is during the height of dogwood season, when the grounds look like a fairyland with delicate white blooms.

Mary Washington House	*Tel. (540)373-1569*
and Garden	*Open: Mar.–Nov., 9–5;*
1204 Charles Street	*Dec.–Feb., 10–4*
Fredericksburg, VA 22401	*Fee*

In 1772 George Washington purchased this house and garden for his mother "to make her more comfortable and free from care." He often visited her there (though he apparently heard many complaints from her about her expenses in maintaining it). Today the restored house and garden are charming. The garden planted by Mrs. Washington is in a typical eighteenth-century style. There are boxwood lined, brick walkways, a sundial still in place, and a vegetable garden separated from a flower garden in the English style. Nearby is an apothecary shop, as well as a historic tavern. This site is not far from Kenmore.

Harrisonburg

The Arboretum at James Madison	*Tel. (540) 568-3194*
University	*Open: daily, dawn to dusk*
(Mailing address: 18 Medical Arts	*Free*
East MSC 5701)	
Harrisonburg, VA 22807	

The University has turned 125 acres of oak-hickory forest into an arboretum with many walking trails, and a series of gardens and natural habitats. There are several striking gardens here; the most extraordinary in spring is one of the state's largest wildflower collections. You'll also see rhododendrons, ferns, and a bog garden. In April the daffodils— more than 50 varieties—and the perennial bulb garden make a great display. In the pond area there are aquatic plants and wildlife to be seen, and another section features a rock garden and herb collection.

Leesburg

Morven Park
41793 Tutt Lane
Leesburg, VA 22075

Tel. (703) 777-2414
Open: April 1–Oct. 31,
Tues.–Sun. 12–5
Free (gardens)

Morven Park is still a working farm with a 1780 Greek Revival mansion and significant gardens. Two noted governors lived here in the nineteenth and early twentieth centuries. The wife of Governor Westmoreland Davis of Virginia planted the gardens. Covering seven acres, they are noted for their enormous boxwood parterre patterns. Called the Marguerite Davis Boxwood Gardens, these formal settings include an elegant reflecting pool and a wide variety of flowers: spring bulbs, June dahlias, and summer annuals. There are notable trees as well: flowering dogwood, crab apple, crape myrtle, Japanese cherry, and magnolias. There are also two self-guided nature trails where you'll see more informal settings with wild flowers.

Oatlands Plantation
20850 Oatlands Plantation Lane
Leesburg, VA 22075

Tel. (703) 777-3174
Open: April–Dec., Mon.–Sat.
10–4:30; Sun. 1–4:30
Fee

Situated in the quiet hills of Virginia's hunt country, Oatlands Plantation is a grand, 1804 Greek Revival mansion surrounded by acres of magnificent terraced gardens overlooking open meadows. The estate—a National Trust for Historic Preservation property—is among the jewels of the Piedmont area, offering historic perspectives on life from the early 1800s through the 1930s, along with one of the most enchanting gardens in the region. Here you can enjoy elaborate interior decors reflecting different styles and periods at the mansion, as well as such garden pleasures as impeccably groomed boxwood parterres, flower gardens, reflecting pools, and elegant statuary.

The site reflects two basically different historic periods and styles: Oatlands as a working plantation in its early days, and Oatlands as a pleasure country retreat in the twentieth century. In 1804 George

Carter, a great grandson of Robert "King" Carter, a wealthy Virginia land baron, designed and built Oatlands House and its gardens on his large property. As with other plantations, the gardens were set near the house to shelter them from the wind. Carter installed a complex series of descending terraces, connected by stone and brick stairways, where he planted fruit trees, vegetables, herbs, flowers, and shrubs. Several acres were dedicated to magnificent English boxwood gardens. To the standard plantation structures—sawmill, gristmill, blacksmith shop, store—he added a large greenhouse, today considered to be the second oldest in the country.

After the Civil War, Oatlands became a refuge for the homeless, then a summer boarding house. At the turn of the century the Carter family, whose fortune had steadily declined, was forced to sell the property, then sadly in shambles. The new owners, the Eustis family, were well connected Washingtonians who used Oatlands as a retreat to pursue their interests, his for fox hunting, hers for gardening. History buffs as well, they restored both house and gardens to their former splendor, infusing some new design ideas in the process. Mrs. Eustis refurbished Carter's gardens, planting new boxwood hedges, a lovely boxwood allée, and flowerbeds with peonies, tulips, iris, and lilies. She also added parterres, statues, a teahouse, bowling green, rose garden, and reflecting pool—all still there, as part of her legacy.

When visiting Oatlands, allow enough time to give the house and its four-and-a-half-acre gardens their due. Before starting out on your garden walk, look over the elegant balustrade for a breathtaking view of the gardens as a whole. From this vantage point, with descriptive leaflets in hand (available at the entrance), you can identify terraces, parterres, flower gardens, and many other delights.

Lorton

Gunston Hall
10709 Gunston Road
Lorton, VA 22079

Tel. (703) 550-9220
Open: daily 9:30–5
Fee

The dignity and eminence of George Mason, author of the Virginia Declaration of Independence and a framer of the United States Constitution, are reflected in Gunston Hall Plantation, his estate for many years. The beautiful brick manor and its surrounding garden, both of which the great statesman designed for himself, are impressive without being in the least showy or pretentious. In its recent restoration, this historic site is a sparkling tribute to classic eighteenth-century style and taste.

Mason began building the house in 1755, on his 5,000-acre tobacco and grain plantation on the shores of the Potomac River. Like much of the colonial tidewater architecture, the house has a simple façade, in contrast with its more elaborate interior, which features baroque carvings and other high-style decorative elements. Mason also had a keen interest in plants, much like his neighbor George Washington at Mount Vernon. He oversaw the management of his plantation himself. Clearly, he was partial to English boxwood, for it is found everywhere at Gunston Hall and includes some of the original plants. The formal gardens include extensive parterres, boxwood hedges, and a magnificent 200-foot long boxwood allée. Now almost 250 years old and 12 feet high, this green avenue is the most historic garden feature here. Gunston Hall is indeed considered to have among the best boxwood green gardens anywhere, England included. Since 1950, these gardens have been maintained by the Garden Club of Virginia. What had become a twentieth-century garden—perhaps by default—regained its historic eighteenth-century style, largely through the efforts of a landscape designer who also worked on the restoration at colonial Williamsburg. Not surprisingly, therefore, there is some resemblance between the two.

The gardens are set within the remaining 550 acres that comprise the plantation. Leading to the house and its surrounding meadows is the welcoming Magnolia Avenue, a double line of magnolias and cedars. Behind are the refurbished formal gardens: the showcase boxwood allée, which forms the main axis from the house to the river, and four elegant parterres, also outlined in boxwood. Two of these parterres feature topiaries, while the other two include rectangular flowerbeds. Beyond, in a less formal arrangement, are cutting gardens, an herb garden, a deer park, and a woodsy nature trail profuse with spring wildflowers, mountain laurels, and dogwoods. The trail leads to the Potomac, about half a mile away where, back in the old days, George Mason's crops would be loaded onto sailing ships for the long voyage to Europe. From this spot you can still enjoy water views and a rich variety of birds.

Manassas

Ben Lomond Manor House
10311 Sudley Manor Drive
Manassas, VA 22110

Email for tourist information:
oldrosegarden@yahoo.com

You may be visiting this famous Civil War site to see the battlefield; if you are also a rose garden enthusiast, make a detour here. This site features a different sort of history; it is a garden devoted to some very ancient rose plantings. Recently bequeathed to the local garden club, this antique rose collection was amassed by a noted rose grower named Jim Syring and replanted here within the last few years. There are some 160 varieties of roses that were grown between the 1400s and 1867, a truly astounding bit of horticultural history.

Montpelier

Montpelier
Route 20 (south of Orange)
Montpelier, VA 22957

Tel. (540) 672-2728
Open: daily 10–4; closed some
holidays
Fee

The elegant Georgian home of President James Madison stands on a 2,700-acre estate, some of which was a land grant of 1723. Its long history includes an 80-year period as a Du Pont family residence, and its acquisition as a National Trust for Historic Preservation site. It was the Du Pont family who laid out the two-acre formal gardens (on the site of earlier gardens) and now they have been beautifully restored. Without original plans, the Garden Club of Virginia undertook to create a typical turn-of-the-century garden. By 1992 twenty different beds had been restored, redesigned, and replenished with spring bulbs. The layout includes the original terraced design of President Madison's time, with a flower-bordered brick entrance wall and gate, and large, crescent-shaped borders.

This is also a place to enjoy unusual trees. There is a self-guided walk with more than 40 varieties of native and non-native trees, including such specialties as the Cedar of Lebanon, the tulip poplar, and the black walnut. Two hundred additional acres have been established as a natural landmark.

Mount Vernon

Mount Vernon	*Tel. (703) 780-2000*
George Washington Memorial	*Open: daily, April–Aug., 8–5;*
Parkway	*March and Sept., 9–5;*
Mount Vernon, VA 22121	*Nov.–Feb., 9–4*
	Fee

Mount Vernon, the legendary home of George Washington, is a serenely green and spacious eighteenth-century plantation overlooking the Potomac. This picturesque site has an elegant aura of history, with its imposing, columned mansion, period exhibits, and scrupulously restored colonial gardens (largely based on Washington's diaries and letters). Not surprisingly, it draws over a million visitors a year, from schoolchildren to foreign tourists to history buffs and—yes—garden lovers. Here you can get a taste of the gracious plantation life of the time and catch a glimpse of the private world of Washington as gentleman farmer and assiduous botanist. But because the grounds are so vast—including some 500 landscaped acres within an extensive property easily four times that size—the crowds are not necessarily intrusive. A self-guided garden walk amid flowers and fruit trees and herbs and boxwood is highly recommended.

Washington's legacy as a gifted gardener and horticulturist—and even landscape designer—lives on at this homesite. The President himself laid out the bowling green, flanked on either side by specimen trees (some of which still exist), serpentine walks, and symmetrical gardens. In keeping with the ideas of balance and perspective embodied in eighteenth century garden design, the bowling green is aligned with both river and mansion. Largely responsible for the gardens' preservation, in as strict accordance with his original plans as possible, has been the Mount Vernon Ladies' Association. The oldest preservation society in the country, it purchased the badly neglected property in 1858, maintaining it to this day.

On one side of the expansive green is the large Upper Garden, a formal composition of flowers, blooming shrubs and trees, and boxwood. Among the flowers (though unspecified in Washington's writings) is a typical eighteenth-century mix including heliotrope, foxglove, pansies, bloodroot, larkspur, and Canterbury bells, set in alternating patterns with vegetables. Espaliered fruit trees against brick walls and boxwood hedges, both favorites of Washington's, are also found here. Some of the boxwood was actually rooted by Washington himself and has been carefully nurtured ever since. A dwarf box parterre features a fleur de lis pattern, a popular design in many eighteenth-century French gardens.

The Lower Garden, entered through a boxwood arch from the south side of the bowling green, is a less formal kitchen garden. Here, on two terraced levels surrounded by brick walls, are herb-bordered geometric vegetable beds featuring more than 30 varieties, and yet more espaliered trees—figs, apples, pears, peaches, and, of course, cherries. There is a deliciously heady aroma from all of these herbs and fruits. There is also a picturesque beehouse, based on early designs.

A third restored garden area is the Botanical Garden. This spot was used for experimenting on imported seeds and plants. If you're interested in botany you will find it intriguing. In addition to these gardens, there are numerous lovely walks among the beauties of Mount Vernon's landscape overlooking the river.

Norfolk

Norfolk Botanical Garden
6700 Azalea Garden Road
Norfolk, VA 23518

Tel. (757) 441-5830
Open: daily, April 15–Oct. 15,
9–7; Oct. 16–April 14, 9–5
Fee

This is one of the most satisfying public gardens we have visited. Not only is the overall arrangement graceful, spacious, and inviting in all its many parts, but each element is well designed and lovely to walk through. From the long row of artistic statuary surrounding a great mowed lawn bordered with flowers, to its wooded gardens of rhododendrons and camellias, and its lovely lines of flowering fruit trees, this is truly a pleasure garden. It has been ranked by the AAA as one of the 10 best gardens in the country.

The gardens are situated very near the water, overlooking both a daffodil-bordered canal that is home to many waterfowl, and two pretty lakes, Lake Whitehurst and Mirror Lake near the Norfolk waterfront. In fact, the site was once known as "Gardens by the Sea," and there is a definite sea breeze as you walk through it, above the shorelines. The nearby airport is almost adjacent; if you bring your children here you'll have a variety of striking views to show them, in addition to the gardens. You can also take a "trackless" train ride or a canal boat through the site.

This botanical garden of about 155 acres of plantings was originally a WPA project. It began with some 4,000 azalea bushes in 1938 (and now numbering a quarter of a million).

Over the years the garden developed into a series of some 20 distinct theme areas, but the overall impression is woodsy throughout. The hand of Charles Gillette, the noted garden designer, can be seen in the care taken here.

Among our favorite features is the Renaissance Court. This spacious garden has several different levels, with ornamental walls and balustrades open on each level, and a semi-circular reflecting pool. It is a masterpiece of garden design, representing the classic style of Italian Renaissance gardens of the late sixteenth century. Adjacent is another unusually lovely spot, the Statuary Vista (mentioned above). Two long rows of tall evergreen hedge with flowerbeds below are punctuated by a series of nineteenth-century marble statues (by Sir Moses Ezekiel) representing the great European artists. You will seldom see a more enchanting combination of art and nature.

Other specialty gardens include a Bog Garden, a Japanese Garden, an award-winning Rose Garden, a Colonial Herb Garden, a Butterfly Garden, a wildflower meadow, and a Healing Garden with a collection of shade plantings with healing properties. When we visited in spring (naturally) the dazzling azaleas and rhododendrons (150 varieties) were fully abloom. (Since the 1950s the International Azalea Festival—honoring NATO—is held here.) And of course there are perennials galore: 25,000 tulips in spring, and more than 50,000 annuals flowering in summer. You'll find 300 varieties of camellias in the woodsy landscape blooming during fall and winter months, and a vast holly collection too. There are 12 miles of trails, and a gazebo, terraces, and occasional benches for reflection. No matter what your special garden interest, you won't be disappointed.

Richmond

Agecroft Hall
4305 Sulgrave Road
Richmond, VA 23221

Tel. (804) 353-4241
Open: Mon.–Sat. 10–4; Sun. 2–5
Fee

This house and garden truly seem to carry the visitor back in time—not just to colonial taste or to the nineteenth-century "gardenesque," but to Tudor and Stuart times in an England transposed to Virginia. Every stone of the elegant house, Agecroft Hall, was rescued from wrecking in Lancashire, England, and brought to this pretty setting by a Virginia businessman named T.C. Richards. The house was reconstructed here on a picturesque riverfront of Richmond in 1928.

The 23-acre gardens, at the house level and on a sloping hillside down to the James River, were designed to maintain the Tudor atmosphere, and are no doubt much as the originals might have looked to a seventeenth-century Englishman and his lady, out for a stroll. There are picture-perfect grounds, green hillside lawns, elms and magnolias, and, best of all, a set of semi-formal gardens and walkways that are both charming and curious. These "pleasure" gardens are especially inviting in springtime; each garden "room" is outlined in boxwood hedge and accented with small statuary and seasonal flowers.

Agecroft's gardens represent an era when gardening was done both for pleasure and with purpose. You begin your tour here with an almost fully enclosed courtyard, which is equipped with seventeenth-century tools used for farming and other Tudor chores. The first of the pleasure garden rooms is a fragrance garden—the nearest to the house, so that its sweet odors presumably would waft through the open leaded windows. Among the many (identified) flowers whose scent and very names are intriguing are the pheasant's eye narcissus, the heliotrope, and the gillyflower. Next is the sunken garden with a raised pond, a replica of one at Hampton Court and truly a pleasure garden both in design and color. Lilies and iris are planted here and there, giving a sense of perfect harmony in this enclosed garden room.

A particularly intriguing walkway, bordered by 50-year-old crape myrtle trees with their gnarled and graceful branches, edges the similarly pale-colored path. Tudor-style shelters from the sun add charm to this odd and pleasing connecting link to the knot garden. This traditional part of early gardens is a formal, enclosed area in which patterns are created by the plantings themselves. This is undoubtedly one of the best knot gardens we've visited. Radishes, lettuce and cabbage crisscross through one bed. In another, various herbs form the patterns. Colored stone and crimson barberry create color contrast. What an amusing way to grow food!

Another highlight is the garden named for John Tradescant, an English botanist who first came to Virginia in 1637 to collect American plant specimens. Surrounded by walls with espaliered pear trees are many rare and exotic plants. And bordering this garden is the herb garden, with some 85 types of herbs used for medicine or cooking. Nearby are a still house where the herbs were dried, and several beehives woven of rye, bulrush, and cattails. You can almost imagine yourself puttering about in the seventeenth century, a recipe book of herbs and honey in hand.

These six garden rooms comprise the formal part of the grounds, but there are also a cutting garden, and a serpentine path through a sloping landscape dotted with flowers, ferns, and woodland, which leads the stroller to the riverbank.

Bryan Park Azalea Gardens　　*Tel. (804) 780-5712*
Hermitage Road and Bellevue　　*Open: daily, dawn to dusk*
*　Avenue*　　*Free*
Richmond, VA 22327

Fifty thousand azalea plants on 20 acres and some 600 white dogwoods are the major attractions here. Needless to say, this is a place to see in springtime. We recommend telephoning in advance to find out the perfect week to visit—between mid-April and mid-May. (Some 200,000 visitors are expected each year.) Among the most popular features is a huge, 35-foot red and white azalea cross, and there are about 50 species of azaleas abloom at the same time. The rest of the park is also quite pretty, with camellias, magnolias, crab apples, American hollies, and many other types of flowering plants, but if it's azaleas and dogwoods you particularly want to see, plan accordingly.

Lewis Ginter Botanical Garden　　*Tel. (804) 262-9887*
1800 Lakeside Avenue　　*Open: daily 9:30–4:30, except*
Richmond, VA 23228　　*　major holidays*
　　Fee

This 90-acre botanical garden bordering a small lake is fairly new (1984). So far 15 acres have been developed, but the site was undergoing much construction when we visited. There are a number of imposing buildings and lots of water here, many new bright pink stone and brick paths, and a series of individual gardens, rather than an overall design. Its most impressive, newly built area is the Asian garden, with water running gently over rocks, and a nice Japanese teahouse. There are numerous additional areas, including a children's educational garden, narcissus and daylily collections, and more than 850 varieties of daffodils. Great care has been taken throughout to label all plants, and many educational programs are offered.

Maymont	*Tel. (804) 358-7166*
1700 Hampton Street	*Open: daily, April–Oct., 10–7;*
Richmond, VA 23220	*Nov.–March, 10–5*
	Free

Lucky Richmond residents have this very beautiful 100-acre park with extensive gardens to visit all year round at no charge. This is indeed a treasure, with both a large and inviting park and a series of exquisite gardens. Its Italianate Garden is surely one of the most inviting formal gardens anywhere in the East, with its natural setting on a cliff above a stream and an equally enchanting Japanese garden, with the James River just beyond.

Maymont was a dairy farm when purchased by Major and Mrs. James Dooley. The elaborate Victorian Romanesque mansion they built was finished in 1893; it took 30 years to complete the magnificent gardens. Having traveled abroad extensively, the Dooleys had clear ideas about what they wanted, and when Maymont's gardens were finished, the estate became a noted showplace. For here were many of the best worldwide garden features recreated in a natural setting of uncommon beauty. In addition to the Italian and Japanese Gardens, there are also a European Grotto Garden, a daylily collection, an herb garden, and an arboretum, as well as vast fields and lawns and stony bluffs. You can visit the house, a carriage house, and a Children's Farm as well.

The Italianate Garden, completed in 1910, is the pièce de résistance. In a natural setting atop a cliff, it has several levels with a 200-foot-long antique columned, wisteria-covered pergola, parterres and terraces, fountains and Renaissance statuary. In between these formal divisions is a profusion of flowers (tulips, candytufts, roses, osmanthus, and many many perennials and annuals) surrounded by clipped evergreens. This is a place to spend precious hours—whether exploring the horticultural or antique aspects, or merely enjoying the picturesque design or the dramatic view of the deep ravine below. This entire site has a sense of the garden as part of its overall environment, not just as a formal work of art. Each garden fits into its setting in such a natural way that it is hard to imagine what was already growing and what was planted specifically for the site. This is particularly true where the steep rocky hillside descends to the six-acre Japanese Stroll Garden. Taking a delightful, very steep, winding stone staircase down, the visitor comes upon the serpentine stream and stepping stones and raked sand of the formal Asian garden. This lovely spot has a tree-shaded teahouse amid small koi ponds, and a spectacular highpoint—a 42-foot-high waterfall.

Other pleasures include the grotto with its mysterious rocky setting, more than 100 varieties of daylilies, and quite an extensive arboretum. There are more than 200 trees here, including many rare and exotic species planted by the Dooleys almost 100 years ago. Don't visit Richmond without seeing Maymont!

Virginia House　　　　　　　　*Tel. (804) 353-4251*
4301 Sulgrave Road　　　　　*Open: Tues.–Sun. 10–4*
Richmond, VA 23221　　　　　*Fee*

This garden fairly takes your breath away. Not just because of the heady aroma of thousands of blooms, among them a glorious rose garden, but because it is so aesthetically lovely. Virginia House, a big, rather gloomy mansion reconstructed stone by stone in 1925 from its English incarnation as a twelfth-century priory called St. Sepulchre, is virtually surrounded by gardens of contrastingly bright, light, colorful flowers. These are divided into garden rooms, called "pleasances," mostly walled, and one more delightful than the next.

Everything here is pale lavenders and pink, rose, and jasmine. We were truly enchanted by the variety and design. The creators of these gardens (landscape architect Charles Gillette, known for his designs in the "picturesque" style, and Virginia Weddell) had a real eye for color, proportion, and line, as well as an interest in rare plants and exotic trees. More modern additions retain a similar style. Gillette is sometimes called the "Interpreter of Southern Gardens," and in fact, he created one here that is quintessentially Southern in its old-world charm. Take your time; anyone who ever planned a garden will appreciate the sleight-of-hand demonstrated at this site.

Your tour of the garden (on your own with map in hand or with a guide) begins at the terrace behind the house. From this spot, you'll have an expansive view of the estate and the water beyond, and you'll get a feeling for the overall design. The alignment of a distant pergola, a canal, pools, and sundial with garden walls and planting demonstrates the strong east-west axis (in contrast with the north-south axis of the staircase to the house and the downhill path). This carefully planned arrangement suggests the European stylistic origins of Virginia House's landscape.

The first garden we visit is the water garden. This enchanting spot is fashioned after one designed by Gertrude Jekyll and Edwin Luytens in Berkshire, England. The use of water, running in an east-to-west canal, is one of the most appealing of any water garden we've seen. Instead of the ubiquitous floating lilies in stagnant ponds of so many water gardens, this one includes a rectangular court enclosed by boxwood and a low brick wall. Within the water are clumps of Japanese iris, sagittaria, and pink and white lotus flowers, all blooming successively. The effect is breathtaking, for the combination of geometric design, small statues, and free-form plantings is both graceful and poetic—seemingly cut off from the world.

Each "pleasance" has its own wall surrounding it, and no two are the same. Varied designs are built into them. Here and there they are dotted by statuary, small fountains, a sundial, and antique vases. These walls, like the fine frames on great paintings, add rather than detract from the composition within.

The next two gardens are devoted to perennial beds featuring mixtures of blooming shrubs, flowers, and clinging vines, and a four seasons bed. The latter includes little statues of the seasons; in spring, the unusual combination of waving tulips in a sea of forget-me-nots is original and thoroughly delightful. This is a Victorian garden in the best sense. Next you'll find azalea and laurel collections surrounding a fifteenth-century bird bath, and a rose garden, including several espaliered varieties, enclosed with special openwork walls, so that the air can circulate.

Below the many formal gardens are the wildflower meadow and the bog garden, where some 125 species of plants grow in wetlands, poetically set beneath weeping willows. Beyond is a woodland walk, and then the riverbank. This is one of the outstanding gardens in our book. Don't miss it!

Staunton

Woodrow Wilson Birthplace
   and Gardens
24 North Coalter Street
Staunton, VA 24401

Tel. (540) 885-0897
Open: daily 9–5
Fee

You can be sure that these gardens, restored in 1933 by noted Richmond landscape designer Charles Gillette, are well worth a visit. Often known as the "Interpreter of Southern Gardens," Gillette turned his hand here to the elegant estate where President Wilson was born. There is now a complex of four buildings, including a museum. The gardens are set in an intricate system of terraces and courts, with the center focus on a bowknot parterre garden outlined in boxwood. Work here by the Garden Club of Virginia over the years has created one of the loveliest gardens in Virginia.

Stratford

Stratford Hall Plantation
Route 214, off Route 3
Stratford, VA 22558

Tel. (804) 493-8038
Open: daily 9:30–4:30
Fee

A visit to Stratford Hall Plantation is a step back in history, both in a tour through the ancestral home of two signers of the Declaration of Independence, and Robert E. Lee's birthplace, and in the very thoroughly researched and restored gardens. The Great House, built by Thomas Lee in about 1738, is considered one of the finest examples of early Georgian architecture in the country, and its "Great Hall" one of the most beautiful rooms in America. Today the 1,600-acre site is maintained as an authentic example of a colonial plantation, with spinning and weaving in process, fields cultivated, and a grist mill in operation. The site of this plantation overlooking the Potomac River in the distance, a mile-long vista, is very grand.

The elegant house has two formal gardens, one to each side. Its gardens were reconstructed by two well-known landscape architects in the 1930s, Morley Williams and Arthur Shurcliff. The brick-walled East Garden is based on site archeology, and is thus one of the most authentic early American gardens around. Here you'll find a boxwood maze and delightful flower parterres that have no less than 3,200 boxwoods. The West Garden has eighteenth-century herbs, a kitchen garden, and an orderly arrangement of flowers. There are both wildflowers and formal plantings: a rose garden, espaliered fruit trees, spring and summer annuals, and a variety of other seasonal delights. There are great trees as well: crape myrtles, flowering dogwood, and great old hickory trees that have seen a lot of history at this site.

Surry

Bacon's Castle
Route 10
(P.O. Box 364)
Surry, VA 23883

Tel. (804) 357-5976
Open: April–Oct. (except Mondays), 10–4; Sun. 12–4; March and Nov., weekends only
Fee

Bacon's Castle features one of the oldest restored gardens in the nation; it is authentically restored to the 1680s, based on archeological evidence. The "Castle" was built in 1665 by an Englishman named Arthur Allen, and is the oldest documented brick house in English North America. The Jacobean mansion is also of architectural interest because it is built in an unusual cruciform style with a porch tower in the front, a medieval stair tower in the rear, and curious Flemish-style gables. Its three massive chimneys were a symbol of status. It became known as Bacon's Castle because a group of Nathaniel Bacon's supporters barricaded themselves within for three months during Bacon's Rebellion in 1665.

The garden, originally laid out by Allen's son, has been restored by the Garden Club of Virginia. It is described as "the oldest, largest, most sophisticated, and best preserved seventeenth-century garden in America." The archeological evidence shows that Allen took a certain interest in the garden's design, as well as its functionality, for there are some ornamental touches, as well as the geometric plainness typical of the time. There is a very large, rectangular growing area bounded by a brick wall southwest of the house, with long, raised planting beds. This area is dissected by white sand walkways. Archeological evidence suggests that other growing areas had curving borders, and perhaps little brick seats for viewing the garden.

The restored garden includes a combination of flower and vegetable sections; border beds are filled with fruits, shrubs, and flowers.

Other features are a forcing wall, starting beds, and extensive vegetable plots. This is an interesting and informative place to visit, particularly if you like history and its horticultural discoveries.

While you are in Surry, make a detour to see the Rolfe-Warren House and Smith's Fort Plantation. Here you'll find the general layout of walks and fencing based on archeological research, as well as plantings of perennials, shrubs, and herbs—all reconstructed by noted landscape architect Arthur Shurcliff in the 1930s.

Virginia Beach

Adam Thoroughgood House
1636 Parish Road
Virginia Beach, VA 23455

Tel. (757) 460-0007
Open: Tues.–Sat. 10–5; Sun. 12–5
Fee

This is a tiny, very charming spot tucked away in a quiet neighborhood. The small brick farmhouse was built in the 1680s by Adam Thoroughgood (the descendant of an indentured servant) on land granted by the Crown. The restored house and garden are typical of late seventeenth-century English cottage style and show the simplicity of tidewater life at the time.

The small, but fine, four-and-a-half-acre Tudor-style garden behind the house is divided into two distinct parterre gardens with topiaries in the center of each. Arbors, espaliered fruit trees, topiary shrubs, and flowers are sprinkled throughout the precise geometric design. There are some 5,000 bulbs planted here, as well as an herb garden. Of particular note are the daylily blooms in June.

Williamsburg

Colonial Gardens of Williamsburg
Williamsburg, VA 23187

Tel. (800) 447-8679
Open: daily 9–5
Fee

Colonial Williamsburg is the most famous living restoration of eighteenth-century Virginia. Though you may know of it for its careful recreation of colonial life, landscape architects and horticulturists prize it as well for its fine gardens. Like the well-maintained houses and streets of its 175 acres, the 90 acres of greens and gardens of

Williamsburg are historically restored—delightfully so. The numerous gardens range from intimate, neat, colonial-style flowerbeds behind the townhouses to the elegant grounds of Governor's Palace, to the charming plantings in the graveyard behind the Bruton Parish Church. For anyone with an interest in eighteenth-century garden design, and an appreciation for Virginia's glorious flowering season, Williamsburg is an enthusiast's pleasure. There are no fewer than 90 residential gardens, of which 25 are open to the public daily, with the others visitable by appointment or tour. Be sure to pick up a map at the center before you start.

The English-style colonial garden had a small, formal layout on the half-acre lots assigned by the laws of colonial settlement. In contrast to the frightening wilderness surrounding their colonial towns, the settlers favored carefully planned, rigorously neat gardens. These small plots typically featured bright flowerbeds, vegetable gardens, and fruit tree areas that were part of the overall architecture of the colonial property, including the dependencies and service areas. (Here you will see the espaliered and dwarf fruit trees that look so charming—but that also saved space by growing against the fences.)

The garden sections typically included bright flowerbeds, outlined by English boxwood hedges in geometric patterns. Topiary circles and squares to ornament the hedges are found in some of the gardens, while one can even see an adventurous hen-shaped topiary (in the Bryan Garden across from the Bruton Parish Church); you'll also see dwarf and tree boxwood. One of the best of these geometric gardens is the formal boxwood design at Wythe House. Typically, the flowers in these town gardens included such English favorites as larkspur, hollyhocks, traditional roses, phlox, foxglove, and the colonial specialty, tulips. One of the best tulip gardens is at the Ludwell-Paradise House. But these familiar English flowers were also interspersed with native American plants like dogwood, coreopsis, black-eyed Susans, and redbud. Among the best flower gardens are those behind Carter's Grove Plantation, where 700 acres contain a variety of blooms, vegetables, and herbs.

Don't miss the tremendous variety of trees in Williamsburg; many are as old as the colony. Some were introduced from abroad. The horse chestnut arrived in 1736, the lovely crape myrtle came from China in 1747, and the paper mulberry from the Orient in the mid-eighteenth century. The Carter-Sanders House has a number of notable trees. Flowering shrubs, both native American and imported, are everywhere. The Ludwell-Paradise House is noted for its summer blooming shrubs.

The grounds of the Governor's Palace, in contrast to these more modest gardens, show us the elegance of the Dutch-English traditional style introduced by William and Mary. The landscape gardens here are said to have matched the elegance of the great European estates of the time (to the displeasure of some democratically-minded colonists). Designed in 1713 for Alexander Spotswood, this landscape will make you imagine you are at a Great House in England. Here you'll see a holly maze (bring the kids!), evergreen parterres, a peached hornbeam allée, espaliered fruit trees, and the spectacular formal garden of 16 boxwood diamonds accented with topiary cones at each corner. This picturesque setting is ornamented with urns and benches, as well as spots of color: scilla, periwinkle, daffodils, and hyacinth in spring. Beyond are fields, vegetable and herb plots, a wooded area for deer, a fish pond, and "Falling Gardens."

A pleasant anachronism at Williamsburg is the formal contemporary garden called the Lila Acheson Wallace Garden at the southwest corner of the historic area. Opened in 1986, it has an oblong reflecting pool with perennial borders, statuary, holly in containers, and a lovely pergola.

WASHINGTON, DC

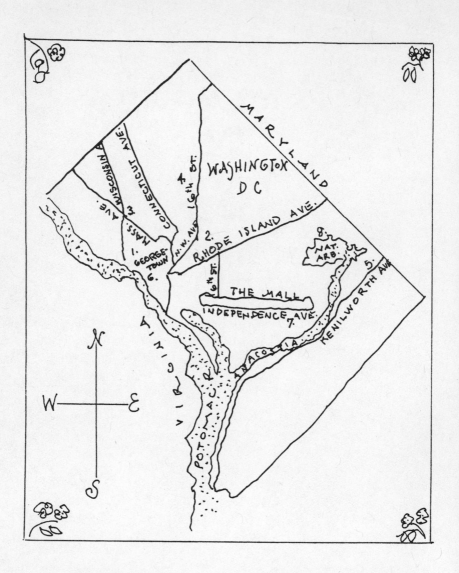

1. Dumbarton Oaks Gardens
2. Franciscan Monastery Gardens
3. Gardens of the Washington
   National Cathedral
4. Hillwood Museum
5. Kenilworth Aquatic Gardens

6. Old Stone House Garden in
   Georgetown
7. United States Botanic Garden
8. United States National
   Arboretum

Dumbarton Oaks Gardens
1703 32nd Street, N.W.
Washington, DC 20007

Tel. (202) 339-6401
Open: April–Nov., daily 2–6
(except Monday);
Nov.–March, 2–5
Fee

In 1921 Robert and Mildred Bliss commissioned the noted landscape gardener Beatrix Jones Farrand to create gardens for their newly purchased mansion, and a masterpiece of American garden design was conceived. The inspired Farrand-Bliss collaboration, based on a mutual admiration of European garden tradition, resulted in the Dumbarton Oaks Gardens. Representing a delightful blend of English, French, and Italian styles within an American landscape, the gardens combine classicism with naturalism in a unique and contemporary—and non-derivative—manner.

The well-traveled and cultivated Farrand had learned her craft through trips to Europe and intense training at Boston's Arnold Arboretum. But her inspirations came in large part from her aunt, the novelist Edith Wharton, herself a garden enthusiast, and the illustrious English landscape gardener Gertrude Jekyll. From Wharton, a key figure in the revival of Italianate gardens in America, she acquired her love of classical gardens; from Jekyll came the emphasis on horticulture over architecture and the idea of garden "rooms," a recurring twentieth-century theme.

Farrand found an ideal partner in Mildred Bliss, an imaginative gardener in her own right. Together, they sought a balance between the traditions of formal European gardens and the natural landscape, a 50-acre property with steeply sloping terrain. Farrand ingeniously devised a scheme of successive formal and naturalistic terraces and enclosures that would allow for distinctive garden segments, each with different design characteristics, planting styles, and architectural ornaments—and degrees of formality. The gardens flow from one to the next in a seamless transition, from very formal, next to the house, to informal, down below. And, though they evoke the Renaissance gardens so admired by Mrs. Bliss—with two main axes extending at right angles from the house, symmetrical fountains, elegant stairways and ornamentation, and broad vistas—they also represent the garden as horticultural delight, focusing on plant colors, shapes, and patterns in the English tradition. Farrand was detail oriented; she carefully planned such elements as patterns of mosaics and stone paths, grass-covered brick steps, shapes of garden beds, and even garden furniture, some of which she designed herself. The 10-acre gardens were completed between 1921 and 1941, with a few additions later on.

At the garden entrance you will be given a carefully prepared and descriptive self-guiding walking tour, which identifies 18 stops of particular interest. You will want to discover and savor each garden room, walkway, and vista at your own pace, lingering at the remarkable views and marveling at the cascades of tumbling forsythia, the romantic wisteria arbors, the graceful courtyards and formal rows of trees and winding steps, the glorious plantings—more than we can describe here.

Some highlights: the Orangerie, a winter garden featuring a climbing fig from the nineteenth century and clusters of potted plants; the Green Garden, affording magnificent views of formal gardens just below; the Beech Terrace, the setting of one of the grandest American beeches we have ever seen; the Urn Terrace, with its beautiful curved pebble mosaic designs; the Rose Garden, a favorite of the Blisses; the Fountain Terrace, its enchanting classical cupid fountains and grassy lawn bordered with colorful bulbs and perennials; Melisande's Allée and Lover's Lane Pool, site of the Roman-style amphitheater; the English-style Herbaceous Border and Vegetable Garden, a feast of color combinations in true Jekyllian tradition; the Ellipse, a group of formally clipped ironwood trees around a small pool with iris; and the magnificent Pebble Garden, an enclosed parterre featuring pebble mosaics in intricate designs and shapes similar to the raised beds of ground cover next to them. The North Vista, a succession of four graceful grass terraces, connected with very gradual brick and grass steps, leads back to the mansion. On your walk you will go up and down the contoured slope, on carefully designed and beautifully kept pathways of stone, brick, and grass.

Franciscan Monastery Gardens   *Tel. (202) 526-6800*
1400 Quincy Street, N.E.   *Open: daily 8 A.M. to dusk*
Washington, DC   *Free*

In a secluded hilltop setting within some 45 wooded acres, these serene gardens embellish the impressive and grand Franciscan Monastery. The 15 acres of well-tended gardens are in two parts: next to the church and cloister are formal flower gardens, and below, amid a naturalistic setting of native shrubs, flowers, trees, and boulders, are evocative recreations of famous religious shrines from the Holy Land.

The commanding yellow brick main church, Rosary Portico, and cloister—all with graceful, rounded arches in an architecture reminiscent of the Spanish Colonial style—date from 1899, but it was not until 1920 that the landscaped gardens were opened to the public. Beautiful rose parterres (including some 2,000 plants) ornament the cloister, along with perennial borders, a small Asian garden near the chapel, and a collection of religious statues (including St. Francis, of course!) framed by geraniums and other blossoms. From these enclosed formal gardens you take a somewhat steep, shaded path that winds around to the quiet valley below. Along the way, in the cool of the deep woods, you'll find the Stations of the Cross enhanced by tall evergreens, magnolias, ferns, ivy, and masses of azaleas and rhododendron. (In spring profusions of blooming bulbs and dogwood add a touch of color.) The path leads to faithful replicas of such spiritual sites as the Grotto of Lourdes, the Grotto of Gethsemane, and the Tomb of Mary, with imposing rock formations and trickling fountains adding to their mysterious ambiance. From a little brick shrine to St. Anne at the bottom of the hill you can enjoy a panorama of meadows with weeping willows, cedars, and magnolias—hardly what you would expect within an urban setting. You will find a visit to these gardens a peaceful and reflective experience.

Gardens of the Washington
 National Cathedral
Massachusetts and Wisconsin
 Avenues, N.W.
Washington, DC 20016

Tel. (202) 537-6200
Open: daily, dawn to dusk
 (Herb Cottage: Mon.–Sat.
 9:30–5; Sun. 10–5)
Free

Any visitor to the nation's capital won't want to miss the imposing National Cathedral, a true Washington landmark, and its famous historic gardens. Consistent with the fourteenth-century-style Gothic cathedral, which was started in 1900 and completed in 1990, the gardens—designed under the guidance of no less than Frederick Law Olmsted, Jr., and Beatrix Jones Farrand, among others—were to contain plants of historical interest, plants of the Bible and Christian legends, and native plants. The formal and informal enclosed gardens are a living museum of biblical and medieval European gardening history.

Before embarking on your gardenwalk, pick up the excellent, descriptive self-guided tour available at the Herb Cottage, which is also a visitor center. You will be surprised to discover how much more complex these intimate gardens actually are than you might think at first glance. Combining unusual architectural features, such as authentic medieval archways, bas reliefs, gates, sculpture with perennial borders, herbaceous plantings in intricate patterns, a rose garden, and flowering shrubs and trees of particular significance (such as cedars and figs), they are a study in symbolism. Among the most evocative is the Bishop's Garden, a medieval garden made up of several tiny parts and created by Olmsted for the bishop's private use. You'll find a Yew Walk (symbolizing immortality), a lower perennial border, a "Hortulus" (small geometric raised beds planted with herbs used in Charlemagne's time), a rose garden (with fragrant floribundas), an herb bed of aromatic and culinary varieties, an old English sundial, a small pool in the shape of a primitive cross, and a stone wall with fifteenth-century bas reliefs of martyrs and saints. Each of these areas invites careful scrutiny. You walk from one garden "room" to the next, along small brick pathways edged with boxwood, its delicate scent permeating the air.

Other garden sites to visit include the Herb Cottage Garden, the woodland pathway bordered with native wildflowers, and the Cloister Garden, featuring a dramatic contemporary bronze fountain. To the west of the cathedral, next to the West Portal Court entrance, is a grove of stately trees, lawns, plantings, walkways, and benches in a parklike setting typical of Olmsted's landscapes. Throughout the grounds are dogwoods, hollies, camellias, azaleas, and other flowering shrubs. There is also a greenhouse specializing in herbs, shade perennials, cacti, and seasonal annuals.

Hillwood Museum
4155 Linnean Avenue, N.W.
Washington, DC 20008

Tel. (202) 686-8500
Open: Tues.–Sat., 11–3; closed in
February
Free (gardens)

This beautifully landscaped site surrounded by deep woods features the elegant mansion and grounds of noted heiress Marjorie Merriweather Post. The Georgian-style house (1920s), which contains Mrs. Post's impressive collection of eighteenth- and nineteenth-century French and Russian fine and decorative arts, became a public museum in 1977, shortly after her death. One glance at the mansion and meticulously groomed gardens, both formal and informal, will tell you that Mrs. Post knew how to live.

Among the garden pleasures are an elegant and formal French parterre with a central pool and fountains; an enchanting rose garden (designed in consultation with landscape architect Perry Wheeler, who also contributed to the White House Rose Garden); a Japanese garden with stream, rocks, pools, and picturesque arched bridges; and a 1930s greenhouse with an important orchid collection. More naturalistic and native plantings include azaleas, rhododendron, dogwood, boxwood, and clusters of trees, some very tall and stately. You can walk around the grounds on your own, though reservations are required for the two-hour house tour.

Kenilworth Aquatic Gardens   *Tel. (202) 426-6905*
1900 Anacostia Drive, S.E.   *Open; daily 8–4*
Washington, DC 20019   *Free*

Peacefully set amid 44 acres of tidal marsh of the Anacostia River, but just a stone's throw from urban bustle, these 12-acre gardens provide a wonderfully naturalistic ambiance in which to view aquatic plants. Maintained by the U.S. Department of the Interior, the specialty gardens feature dozens of ponds filled to capacity with water lilies and lotuses (especially spectacular in June, July, and August), as well as cattails, iris, water primrose, and hyacinth. Grassy (and sometimes muddy) paths circle the ponds, where you might also see turtles, snakes, frogs, migratory waterfowl, and other birds. With walking guide in hand (available at the entrance), you can identify each site.

This national park was once the private waterside garden of Civil War veteran Walter Shaw, who decided to plant water lilies to remind him of his native Maine. From a few specimens the gardens grew and grew, as his daughter Helen traveled around the world in search of more exotic varieties. Helen became proprietor in 1921 and continued to oversee the gardens until her death in 1957. When the property was threatened by a dredging plan along the river, it was sold to the government for preservation. In the last decades the Kenilworth Aquatic Gardens have been dedicated to the propagation of water plants, both native and exotic, and to the preservation of the last natural tidal marsh in Washington.

Old Stone House Garden in
Georgetown
3051 M Street, N.W.
Washington, DC 20019

Tel. (202) 426-6851
Open: Wed.–Sun. 8–4:30
Fee

Behind this charming 1764 fieldstone house, Washington's only sur-
viving pre-Revolutionary building, is a very pretty, old-fashioned garden. The terraced property is graced with fruit trees, perennial flowerbeds in great masses, wild roses, curving lawns, and brick stone paths.
A walk on these intimate grounds is a real pleasure!

You can visit the garden (which is partly visible from the road) and
the house, featuring colonial furnishings and artifacts, on your own;
costumed guides are on hand to answer questions.

United States Botanic Garden
245 First Street S.W.
Washington, DC 20024

Tel. (202) 225-8333
Open: daily, dawn to dusk.
Bartholdi Park open daily,
dawn to dusk; Conservatory
hours to be announced.
Free

The United States Botanic Garden describes itself as a "living museum."
It is, in fact, surrounded by the capital's world-famous museums up
and down the Mall. But it hardly seems like a museum when you visit
it, because you are surrounded by living things—riotous color, delicate shapes, exotic blooms.

The present conservatory—rather charmingly old-fashioned—was
built in 1933 and is now undergoing renovation. When last we visited
there was an extraordinary exhibition of orchids, as well as a Desert
Garden, and splendid fossils. The updated conservatory promises
brand-new displays. In addition, there are outdoor plantings across Independence Avenue from the Conservatory in Frederic Auguste
Bartholdi Park. Named for the famous sculptor, whose historic foundation is the centerpiece, the park features seasonal displays.

United States National Arboretum
3501 New York Avenue, N.E.
Washington, DC 20002

Tel. (202) 245-2726
Open: Mon.–Fri. 8–5; weekends
10–5
Free

The United States National Arboretum is much more than a collection of trees. Here, amid 446 acres of rolling land, are magnificent specialty gardens and collections, many of which are among the best of their kind in the country. The mission of this vast facility, the only federally funded arboretum in the country—is "to conduct research, provide education, conserve and display trees, shrubs, and other plants to enhance the environment." It includes some 37 sites that can be visited (preferably traveling from one to the next by car, given the distances), all labeled and identified. You will drive or walk in a landscape of remarkable trees, ponds, and vistas, seeing important collections of Asian plantings, dwarf conifers, azaleas, hollies, crabtrees, wildflowers, woodland plants, and some spectacular formal gardens. A 48 passenger accessible tram operates on weekends from April through October.

This is an enormous place. Before you start out, pick up a map at the administration center and information/gift shop, numbered according to a suggested route. (The administration center itself contains a huge herbarium with more than 600,000 pressed varieties from all over the world.) A small sign points to the National Bonsai and Penjing Collections and National Herb Garden, without doubt among the most remarkable displays in the Arboretum.

The bonsai compound contains the largest and most complete collection in North America. Here, amid shaded stone and gravel walkways, moon gates, and enchanting little interior gardens, are the fine exhibits, housed in various pavilions and greenhouses. The bonsai on display in the airy Japanese pavilion include some 53 that were presented as a bicentennial gift to the American people. These rare and precious treasures, representing one of Japan's most revered art forms, can reach a venerable old age—one is apparently already more than 360 years old!

The Chinese pavilion displays its Penjing collection, which features plants that have been dwarfed using a different technique from the bonsai. Here, too, are Chinese artifacts, such as large watering jars and stone lanterns, as well as the craggy symbolic rocks and tiny arched bridges and stone paths traditionally found in Chinese gardens.

Directly across the street from the bonsai collection is the wonderful National Herb Garden, the largest designed herb garden in the world. You enter through a walkway of fragrant boxwood; once inside you will want to linger in this ordered world of clipped hedges, graceful trellises, fountains, and plantings in intricate patterns. Beyond is a grand panorama reminiscent of an English romantic landscape, with a broad expanse of meadow framing a group of great columns soaring in the distance. Known as the National Capitol Columns, they were once part of the U.S. Capitol building and were salvaged when the building was renovated in 1957. In 1990 they were placed in the Arboretum under the personal supervision of the noted landscape designer Russell Page, who added a fountain, water stair, and reflecting pool to enhance them.

The Herb Garden is made up of three separate gardens: the Knot Garden, Historic Rose Garden, and the oval specialty gardens. The first is a formal arrangement of dwarf evergreens in interlocking designs surrounding a circular brick terrace and fountain; on each side are arbors covered with clematis and grapevines. The Rose Garden contains specimens of historic interest, many quite rare and of ancient origins; they come from various parts of the world and are all identified. The tiny specialty gardens are all thematic and herbal. Contained within a one-acre grassy oval, they include a garden dedicated to plants listed by the ancient Greeks; a dye garden planted with specimens used in the dyeing of fabric; an early American garden in the colonial tradition; an American Indian garden with herbs used by Native Americans for beverages and medicines and crafts; a medicinal garden; a culinary garden; a wild bird garden; an industrial garden containing plants of economic value (rubber, flax, hops, etc.); a fragrance garden; an Oriental garden; and a beverage garden.

There are many other garden sites to enjoy in the Arboretum, perhaps too many for one visit. If you have limited time, we especially recommend Fern Valley and the Gotelli Dwarf and Slow-Growing Conifer Collection. The first is a naturalistic wonder in a valley of deep woods, tall evergreens, century-old beeches, oaks, and tulip trees, a gentle stream, and meadow garden. The Gotelli Conifer Collection is a rare experience, considered one of the finest such gardens in the world. Magnificent varieties of fir, cedar, juniper, pine, hemlock, spruce, and other specimens are set on five hillside acres. Here is a fascinating assortment of plants in different shapes, textures, and sizes set in well-tended, rounded gravel beds, separated by grassy pathways. Surrounding them are ornamental grasses and bulbs, all carefully identified.

CHOOSING AN OUTING
Authors' Recommendations

*AQUATIC GARDENS AND GARDENS
WITH WATER VIEWS*

Alabama
Bellingrath Gardens
Birmingham Museum of Art
Jasmine Hill Gardens

Florida
Alfred B. Maclay State Gardens
Everglades National Park
Marie Selby Botanical Garden
Rockefeller Gardens
Slocum Water Gardens
Vizcaya
Washington Oaks State Gardens

Georgia
Guido Gardens
Okefenokee Swamp Park
Riverwalk in Augusta
Vines Botanical Gardens

Kentucky
Broadmoor Garden and Conservatory

Louisiana
Longue Vue Gardens

North Carolina.
Greensboro Arboretum
Greensboro Bicentennial Garden
  and Bog Garden
New Hanover County Extension
  Service Arboretum
Orton Plantation Gardens

South Carolina
Edisto Memorial Gardens
Hopeland Gardens

Magnolia Plantation and Gardens
Middleton Place
Swan Lake Iris Gardens

Tennessee
Opryland

Virginia
Norfolk Botanical Garden
Virginia House

Washington, DC
Kenilworth Aquatic Gardens

ARBORETUMS

Florida
Flamingo Garden and Arboretum
Florida Institute of Technology
  Botanical Garden

Georgia
Lockerly Arboretum

Kentucky
Bernheim Arboretum and Research
  Forest
University of Kentucky Arboretum

Mississippi
The Crosby Arboretum

North Carolina
Campus Arboretum of Haywood
  Community College
Greensboro Arboretum
J.C. Raulston Arboretum at N.C.S.U.
New Hanover County Extension
  Service Arboretum

North Carolina Botanical Garden
and Coker Arboretum
Tanglewood Arboretum and Rose
Garden

Virginia
The Arboretum at James Madison
University
Orland E. White Arboretum

Washington, DC
United States National Arboretum

BEST VIEWS

Florida
Bok Tower Gardens

Georgia
Rock City Gardens

North Carolina
Biltmore Estate
Cape Fear Botanical Garden
Sarah P. Duke Gardens

South Carolina
Middleton Place

Virginia
Mount Vernon
River Farm

COMBINING GARDENS WITH ART

Alabama
The Charles W. Ireland Sculpture
Garden (Birmingham Museum
of Art)
Jasmine Hill Gardens

Florida
Cummer Gallery of Art
Coral Castle
Vizcaya

Georgia
Barnsley Gardens

Kentucky
Lexington Cemetery

Louisiana
Rosedown Plantation and Gardens

South Carolina
Brookgreen Gardens

Tennessee
Cheekwood
Dixon Gallery and Gardens

Washington, DC
Dumbarton Oaks Gardens
Hillwood Museum

**CONSERVATORIES AND
BOTANIC GARDENS**

Alabama
Birmingham Botanical Gardens
The Huntsville-Madison County
Botanical Garden
Mobile Botanical Gardens
Noccalula Falls Botanical Gardens

Florida
Eureka Springs Park
Kanapaha Botanical Gardens
Marie Selby Botanical Gardens
McKee Botanical Garden
Mounts Botanical Garden

Georgia
Callaway Gardens
Chatham County Garden Center and
Botanical Gardens
Georgia Perimeter College Botanical
Garden
Vines Botanical Gardens

Louisiana
New Orleans Botanical Garden

North Carolina
The Botanical Gardens at Asheville
Cape Fear Botanical Garden
Daniel Boone Native Gardens
Daniel Stowe Botanical Garden
New Hanover County Extension
  Service Arboretum
Reynolda Gardens at Wake Forest
  University
U.N.C. Charlotte Botanical Gardens

South Carolina
South Carolina Botanical Garden

Tennessee
Memphis Botanic Garden
Reflection Riding
Opryland

Virginia
Agecroft Hall
Green Spring Gardens Park
Lewis Ginter Botanical Garden
Norfolk Botanical Garden

Washington, DC
United States Botanic Garden

FORMAL GARDENS

Alabama
Bellingrath Gardens

Florida
Alfred B. Maclay State Gardens
Ringling Museums and Gardens
Vizcaya

Georgia
Atlanta History Center
Oak Hill at the Martha Berry
  Museum

Kentucky
Ashland

Louisiana
Afton Villa

North Carolina
Airlie Gardens
Orton Plantation Gardens
Reynolda Gardens at Wake Forest
  University

South Carolina
Glencairn Garden
Middleton Place

Tennessee
Dixon Gallery and Gardens

Virginia
Gunston Hall
Maymont
Morven Park

Washington, DC
Dumbarton Oaks Gardens
Franciscan Monastery Gardens
Gardens of the Washington National
  Cathedral

GARDEN "ROOMS"

Florida
Coral Castle

Georgia
Founders Memorial Garden

Louisiana
Afton Villa
Longue Vue Gardens

Tennessee
Dixon Gallery and Gardens

Virginia
Agecroft Hall
Virginia House

Washington, DC
Dumbarton Oaks Gardens

GARDENS THAT CHILDREN WILL ESPECIALLY ENJOY

Alabama
The Huntsville-Madison County
  Botanical Garden
Noccalula Falls Botanical Gardens

Florida
Busch Gardens
Butterfly World
Marie Selby Botanical Gardens
Ringling Museums and Gardens
Sarasota Jungle Gardens
Sunken Gardens

Georgia
Atlanta Botanical Garden
Atlanta History Center
Barnsley Gardens
Callaway Gardens
Oak Hill at the Martha Berry
  Museum
Okefenokee Swamp Park

Kentucky
Broadmoor Garden and
  Conservatory

Louisiana
Jungle Gardens

North Carolina
Daniel Boone Native Gardens
Sandhills Horticultural Gardens
Wilkes Community College Gardens
Wing Haven Gardens and Bird
  Sanctuary

South Carolina
Brookgreen Gardens
Cypress Gardens

Virginia
Agecroft Hall
Maymont
Mount Vernon
Norfolk Botanical Garden
River Farm

GARDENS BY FAMOUS LANDSCAPE DESIGNERS

Florida
Bok Tower Gardens (Frederick Law
  Olmsted)

North Carolina
Biltmore Estate (Frederick Law
  Olmsted)
The Botanical Garden at Asheville
  (Doan Ogden)
Campus Arboretum of Haywood
  Technical College (Doan Ogden)
Daniel Boone Native Gardens (Doan
  Ogden)
Sarah P. Duke Gardens (Ellen Biddle
  Shipman)

Virginia
Monticello (Thomas Jefferson)
Norfolk Botanical Garden (Charles
  Gillette)
Pavilion Gardens, University of
  Virginia (Thomas Jefferson)
Virginia House (Gertrude Jekyll)
Woodrow Wilson Birthplace and
  Garden (Charles Gillette)

Washington, DC
Dumbarton Oaks Gardens (Beatrix
  Farrand)
Gardens of the Washington National
  Cathedral (Beatrix Farrand)

GARDENS OF HISTORIC HOUSES AND PLANTATIONS

Alabama
Arlington House and Garden

Georgia
Richardson-Owens-Thomas House
  and Gardens

Louisiana
Rosedown Plantation and Gardens
Shadows-on-the-Teche

Mississippi
Florewood River Plantation State
Park
Monmouth Plantation
Rosemont Plantation

North Carolina
Orton Plantation Gardens
Tryon Palace Gardens

South Carolina
Boone Hall Plantation
Boylston Gardens
Magnolia Plantation and Gardens
Robert Mills House

Virginia
Berkeley Plantation
Monticello
Mount Vernon
Oak Ridge Estate
Oatlands Plantation
Preswould Plantation
Stratford Hall Plantation
Woodlawn Plantation

GARDENS OF
NOTABLE AMERICANS

Florida
Edison-Ford Winter Estates (Henry
Ford and Thomas Edison)
Rockefeller Gardens (John D.
Rockefeller)

Kentucky
Ashland (Henry Clay)

Louisiana
Live Oaks Gardens (Joseph
Jefferson)

Mississippi
Beauvoir (Jefferson Davis)
Rosemont Plantation (Jefferson
Davis)
Rowan Oak (William Faulkner)

South Carolina
Brookgreen Gardens (Anna Hyatt
Huntington and Archer
Huntington)
Middleton Place (Henry Middleton)

Tennessee
Blount Mansion (William Blount)
The Hermitage (Andrew Jackson)

Virginia
Ashlawn-Highland (James Monroe)
Gunston Hall (George Mason)
Kenmore (Col. Fielding Lewis)
Monticello (Thomas Jefferson)
Montpelier (James Madison)
Mount Vernon (George Washington)
Oak Ridge Estate (Thomas Fortune
Ryan)
Pavilions at University of Virginia
(Thomas Jefferson)
Stratford Hall (Robert E. Lee)
Woodrow Wilson Birthplace and
Garden (Woodrow Wilson)

Washington, DC
Hillwood Museum (Marjorie
Merriweather Post)

GARDENS REFLECTING
AMERICAN HISTORY

Georgia
Founders Memorial Garden

Kentucky
Shaker Village of Pleasant Hill

Louisiana
Shadows-on-the-Teche
Ursuline Convent

Mississippi
Monmouth Plantation

North Carolina
Biltmore Estate
Elizabethan Gardens

Old Salem
Tryon Palace Gardens

South Carolina
Boone Hall Plantation
Middleton Place

Tennessee
Blount Mansion

Virginia
Adam Thoroughgood House
Agecroft Hall
Bacon's Castle
Berkeley Plantation
Gunston Hall
Kenmore
Mary Washington House and Garden
Monticello
Montpelier
Mount Vernon
Oatlands
Pavilions at University of Virginia
Prestwould
Stratford Hall
Williamsburg Colonial Gardens
Woodlawn Plantation

Washington, DC
Old Stone House in Georgetown

*GARDENS WITH
UNUSUAL THEMES*

Florida
Fruit and Spice Park

Georgia
Atlanta Botanical Garden (garden of
  carnivorous plants)
Guido Gardens (garden for
  Evangelical broadcasts)
Oak Hill at the Martha Berry
  Museum (goldfish garden)

Mississippi
Palestinian Gardens

*INFORMAL AND
ENGLISH-STYLE GARDENS*

Georgia
Oak Hill at the Martha Berry
  Museum

Louisiana
Afton Villa
Hodges Gardens

Mississippi
Beauvoir
Mynelle Gardens
Wister Gardens

North Carolina
Airlie Gardens
Biltmore Estate

South Carolina
Brookgreen Gardens
Hatcher Gardens
Magnolia Plantation and Gardens

Tennessee
The Hermitage

Virginia
Virginia House

Washington, DC
Dumbarton Oaks Gardens
Franciscan Monastery Gardens
Gardens of Washington National
  Cathedral

ITALIANATE GARDENS

Florida
Cummer Gallery of Art
Vizcaya

Georgia
Atlanta History Center
Barnsley Gardens

North Carolina
Biltmore Estate

Virginia
Maymont
Norfolk Botanical Garden

Washington, DC
Dumbarton Oaks Gardens

MAJOR ASIAN GARDENS

Alabama
Bellingrath Gardens

Florida
Four Arts Garden
Morikami Park

Georgia
Atlanta History Center
Riverwalk (Augusta)
Vines Botanical Gardens

North Carolina
Sarah P. Duke Gardens

South Carolina
Swan Lake Iris Gardens

Tennessee
Cheekwood
Memphis Botanic Garden

Virginia
Lewis Ginter Botanical Garden
Maymont

Washington, DC
United States National Arboretum

MEDICINAL AND HERB GARDENS

Georgia
State Botanical Garden of Georgia

Kentucky
Shaker Village of Pleasant Hill

Mississippi
Mynelle Gardens

North Carolina
Old Salem Gardens
Wing Haven Gardens and Bird
   Sanctuary

Virginia
Agecroft Hall
Colonial Gardens of Williamsburg
River Farm

Washington, DC
United States National Arboretum

ROCK GARDENS

Alabama
Bellingrath Gardens
Birmingham Botanical Gardens

Georgia
Atlanta History Center
Barnsley Gardens
Rock City Gardens

Louisiana
Hodges Gardens

Virginia
The Arboretum at James Madison
   University

ROMANTIC GARDENS

Alabama
Jasmine Hill Gardens

Florida
Harry P. Leu Gardens
Vizcaya

Georgia
Barnsley Gardens
Cator Woolford Memorial Garden

Louisiana
Afton Villa
Longue Vue Gardens

North Carolina
Airlie Gardens

South Carolina
Glencairn Garden
Middleton Place

Virginia
Oak Ridge Estate

Washington, DC
Dumbarton Oaks Gardens

ROSE GARDENS

Alabama
Bellingrath Gardens

Georgia
Robert L. Staton Rose Garden

Louisiana
The Gardens of the American Rose
    Center
New Orleans Botanical Garden
Rosedown Plantation and Gardens

North Carolina
Biltmore Estate
Raleigh Municipal Rose Garden
Tanglewood Rose Garden and
    Arboretum

South Carolina
Edisto Memorial Gardens

Virginia
Ben Lomond Manor House
Norfolk Botanical Garden
Woodlawn Plantation

Washington, DC
Dumbarton Oaks Gardens

SITES FEATURING BIRDS
AND OTHER ANIMALS

Alabama
Noccalula Falls Botanical Garden

Florida
Busch Gardens
Butterfly World
Caribbean Gardens
Everglades National Park
Flamingo Gardens and Arboretum
Sunken Gardens

Kentucky
Broadmoor Garden and
    Conservatory

Louisiana
Jungle Gardens

North Carolina
Orton Plantation
Wing Haven Garden and Bird
    Sanctuary

THE SOUTH'S MAJOR GARDENS

Alabama
Bellingrath Gardens

Florida
Florida Cypress Gardens
Vizcaya

Georgia
Callaway Gardens

North Carolina
Biltmore Estate
Elizabethan Gardens
Orton Plantation Gardens
Sarah P. Duke Gardens

South Carolina
Magnolia Plantation and Gardens
Middleton Place

Virginia
Colonial Gardens of Williamsburg
Gunston Hall

Maymont
Monticello
Mount Vernon
Norfolk Botanical Garden

Washington, DC
Dumbarton Oaks Gardens

SPECIALTY GARDENS
(also see ROSE GARDENS, above)

Florida
Harry P. Leu Gardens (camellias)
Marie Selby Botanical Gardens
  (orchids)
Orchid Jungle (orchids)
Sunken Gardens (orchids)

Georgia
Callaway Gardens (azaleas)
Fred Hamilton Rhododendron
  Garden (rhododendrons)
Massee Lane Camellia Gardens
  (camellias)

Louisiana
Zemurray Gardens (azaleas)

North Carolina
Greenfield Gardens (azaleas)
J.C. Raulston Arboretum at N.C.S.U.
  (redbud trees)
Sandhills Horticultural Gardens
  (holly)

South Carolina
Glencairn Garden (azaleas)
Kalmia Gardens of Coker College
  (mountain laurel)
Swan Lake Iris Gardens (Japanese
  iris)

Tennessee
Cheekwood (trillium)

Virginia
Bryan Park (azaleas)
Gunston Hall (boxwood)

Norfolk Botanical Garden
  (camellias)
Orland E. White Arboretum
  (boxwood)

TOPIARY GARDENS

Florida
Vizcaya

South Carolina
Magnolia Plantation and Gardens

Virginia
Adam Thoroughgood House
Gunston Hall
Colonial Gardens of Williamsburg

TROPICAL, SUBTROPICAL,
AND SWAMP GARDENS

Florida
Caribbean Gardens
Cluett Memorial Garden
Everglades National Park
Fairchild Tropical Garden
Florida Cypress Gardens
Four Arts Garden
Orchid Jungle
Ravine State Gardens
Sarasota Jungle Gardens
Simpson Park Hammock
Sunken Gardens

Louisiana
Jungle Gardens

South Carolina
Cypress Gardens
Magnolia Plantation and Gardens

Tennessee
Opryland

Washington, DC
Kenilworth Aquatic Gardens

URBAN SETTINGS

Florida
Simpson Park Hammock

Georgia
Forsyth Park
Riverwalk (Augusta)

North Carolina
N.C. Botanical Garden and Coker
   Arboretum (Chapel Hill)
Raleigh Municipal Rose Garden

South Carolina
Boylston Gardens
Hampton Park
Memorial Garden

Washington, DC
Gardens of the National Cathedral
Old Stone House Garden in
   Georgetown

WILDFLOWERS AND WOODLANDS

Mississippi
The Crosby Arboretum

North Carolina
Sarah P. Duke Gardens

South Carolina
Brookgreen Gardens
Hatcher Gardens

Tennessee
Reflection Riding

Virginia
The Arboretum at James Madison
   University
Morven Park
Norfolk Botanical Garden
Prestwould Plantation